THE MYSTICAL LORE OF PRECIOUS STONES

THE MYSTICAL LORE OF

PRECIOUS STONES

Being a Combination of Two Histories, "The Curious Lore of Precious Stones," 1913, and "The Magic of Jewels and Charms," 1915

VOLUME II

THE CLASSIC WRITINGS OF
GEORGE FREDERICK KUNZ
A.M., PH.D., D.SC.

ILLUSTRATED

NEWCASTLE PUBLISHING CO., INC.
NORTH HOLLYWOOD, CALIFORNIA
1986

Volume I: ISBN 0-87877-094-1
Volume II: ISBN 0-87877-095-4

A Newcastle Gem and Crystal Classic
First Paperback Printing August 1986
9 8 7 6 5 4 3 2 1
Printed in the United States of America

WITH HEARTFELT APPRECIATION OF THE NOBLE SPIRIT THAT CONCEIVED AND FOUNDED THE MORGAN-TIFFANY COLLECTION OF GEMS AND THE MORGAN-BEMENT COLLECTIONS OF MINERALS AND METEORITES OF THE AMERICAN MUSEUM OF NATURAL HISTORY, AND THE MORGAN COLLECTION OF THE MUSÉE D'HISTOIRE NATURELLE OF PARIS, AND WHOSE KINDLY ADVICE AND ENCOURAGEMENT HAVE DONE SO MUCH FOR THE PRECIOUS STONE ART, THIS VOLUME IS RESPECTFULLY DEDICATED TO THE MEMORY OF THE LATE

J. PIERPONT MORGAN

Preface

THE love of precious stones is deeply implanted in the human heart, and the cause of this must be sought not only in their coloring and brilliancy but also in their durability. All the fair colors of flowers and foliage, and even the blue of the sky and the glory of the sunset clouds, only last for a short time, and are subject to continual change, but the sheen and coloration of precious stones are the same to-day as they were thousands of years ago and will be for thousands of years to come. In a world of change, this permanence has a charm of its own that was early appreciated.

The object of this book is to indicate and illustrate the various ways in which precious stones have been used at different times and among different peoples, and more especially to explain some of the curious ideas and fancies that have gathered around them. Many of these ideas may seem strange enough to us now, and yet when we analyze them we find that they have their roots either in some intrinsic quality of the stones or else in an instinctive appreciation of their symbolical significance. Through manifold transformations this symbolism has persisted to the present day.

The same thing may be said in regard to the various superstitions connected with gems. Our scientific knowledge of cause and effect may prevent us from accepting any of the fanciful notions of the physicians and astrologers of the olden time; nevertheless, the possession of a necklace or a ring adorned with brilliant diamonds, fair pearls, warm, glowing rubies, or celestial-hued sapphires will to-day make a woman's heart beat faster and bring a blush of pleasure to her cheek. Life will seem better worth living to her; and, indeed, this is no delusion, for life is what our thought makes it, and joy is born of gratified desire. Hence nothing that contributes to increasing the sum of innocent pleasures should be disdained; and surely no pleasure can be more innocent and justifiable than that inspired by the possession of beautiful natural objects.

The author, who possesses what is believed to be the most comprehensive private library on this subject, has obtained many references from material which he has been gathering during the past twenty-five years. Many of the types exist in the collection of folk-lore precious stones exhibited at the World's Columbian Exposition in 1893, and now in the Field Museum of Natural History in Chicago. Other types are drawn from the Morgan Collection exhibited at the Paris Expositions of 1889 and 1900, which, with additions, is now in Morgan Hall, in the American Museum of Natural History, New York City.

Other prominent references are the collection of precious stones in the California Midwinter Memorial Museum, in Golden Gate Park, San Francisco; the Tiffany collection of precious stones, exhibited at the Atlanta Exposition of 1894, now in the National Museum in Washington; the collection exhibited at the Pan-American Exposition, and presented to the Musée d'Histoire Naturelle, in Paris, by the late J. Pierpont Morgan; the collection exhibited at the exposition held in Portland, Oregon, in 1905; and the collection of gems and precious stones exhibited at the Jamestown Exposition, 1907. All of these collections, either entirely or very largely, have been formed by the author.

Some references to sentiment connected with precious stones are embodied in the little work, now in its 21st edition, entitled: "Natal Stones, Sentiments and Superstitions Associated with Precious Stones," compiled by the writer, who has examined nearly all the principal collections in the United States, Europe, Mexico, Canada, and Asiatic Russia.

For courtesies, information and illustrations, I am indebted to the following, to whom my thanks are due:

Prof. Taw Sein Ko, Superintendent of the Archæological Survey, of Burma; Dr. T. Wada, of Tokyo, Japan; Dr. G. O. Clerc, President of the Société Ouralienne des Amis des Sciences Naturelles, Ekaterinebourg, Russia; Dr. Charles Braddock, late Medical Inspector to the King of Siam; Sir Charles Hercules Reed, Curator of Archæology, and Dr. Ernest A. Wallis Budge, Egyptologist, British Museum, London; A. W. Feavearyear, Esq., London; Dr. Salomon Reinach, Director of the Archæological Museum of St. Germain-en-Laye, France; Prof. Giuseppe Belucci, of the University of Perugia; Dr. Peter Jessen, Librarian of the Kunstgewerbe Museum, of Berlin; Miss Belle DaCosta Green; Dr. Frederick Hirth, Chinese Professor, Columbia University, New York; Dr. Clark Wissler, Curator of Archæology, Dr. L. P. Gratacap, Curator of Mineralogy, American Museum of Natural History; Dr. Berthold Laufer, Oriental Archæologist, and Dr. Oliver C. Farrington, Curator of Geology and Mineralogy, Field Museum of Natural History, Chicago; Hereward Carrington, Esq., Psychist, New York; Dr. W. Hayes Ward, Archæologist and Babylonian Scholar; Mrs. Henry Draper, New York; H. W. Kent, Esq., Metropolitan Museum of Art, New York City; Consul General Moser, Colombo, Ceylon; W. W. Blake, Mexico City, who has done so much to encourage Mexican archæological investigation; the late A. Damour, of Paris, the great pioneer of mineralogical archæology; the late Dr. A. B.

Meyer, of Dresden, who, more than anyone else, proved that the *Nephritfrage* or the jade question was to be solved by chemical and mineralogical investigation; the late Rajah Sir Sourindro Mohun Tagore, of Calcutta; and Dr. A. M. Lythgoe, Egyptologist, Metropolitan Museum of Art.

G. F. K.

SEPTEMBER, 1913.

Contents

Volume I Describes:

- Superstitions and their Sources,
- Use of Precious and Semi-precious Stones as Talismans and Amulets,
- Talismanic Use of Special Stones,
- Use of Engraved and Carved Gems as Talismans,
- Ominous and Luminous Stones.

I

Religious Uses of Precious Stones, Pagan, Hebrew, and Christian

THE use of stones for the decoration of images of the gods, and in religious ceremonies, more especially in those connected with the burial of the dead, can be traced back to a remote antiquity. Indeed, we may regard this religious use of precious or peculiar stones as the natural development of the original idea of their talismanic virtue. If a certain supernatural essence manifested itself in the stone, what more fit object could be imagined for the decoration of statues of the gods, or to bear engraved texts from the sacred writings, and to be placed with the bodies of the dead as "passports" to ensure the safe entry of the souls of the departed into the better land?

While this employment of mineral substances for religious purposes is practically universal, the earliest recorded instances come from Egypt, and concern the Egyptian custom of engraving texts from a very ancient ritual composition, called the Book of the Dead, upon certain semi-precious stones which had been cut into various symbolical forms. This "Book of the Dead," composed of a number of distinct chapters, each complete in itself, describes the passage of the soul of the deceased through the realm of the dead (Amenti). Here the soul addresses the gods and other beings who receive it, and the prayers and invocations recited in the chapters are supposed to procure a safe passage and protection from all evil influences or impediments.

One of the most usual of the engraved amulets is the buckle or tie (thet). This was generally of red jasper, carnelian, or red porphyry, or else of red glass or faience or of sycamore wood. The wood was symbolical of the blood of Isis, and the amulets were sometimes engraved with the 156th chapter of the Book of the Dead; they were placed on the mummy's neck. The formula engraved reads:

> Chapter of the buckle of carnelian which is put on the neck of the deceased.
>
> The blood of Isis, the virtue of Isis; the magic power of Isis, the magic power of the Eye are protecting this the Great one; they prevent any wrong being done to him.
>
> This chapter is said on a buckle of carnelian dipped into the juice of ankhama, inlaid into the substance of the sycamore-wood and put on the neck of the deceased.
>
> Whoever has this chapter read to him, the virtue of Isis protects him; Horus, the son of Isis, rejoices in seeing him, and no way is barred to him, unfailingly.[1]

Another amulet is the *tet*. The hieroglyph represents a mason's table and the word signifies "firmness, stability, preservation." These figures, made of faience, gold, carnelian, lapis-lazuli, and other materials, were placed on the neck of the mummy to afford protection.[2]

The "papyrus scepter," *uat*, is usually cut from matrix-emerald or made of faience of similar hue. *Uat* means "verdure, flourishing, greenness"; placed on the neck of the mummy it was regarded as emblematic of the

---

[1] Life Work of Sir Peter le Page Renouf, Paris, 1907, vol. iv, p. 342. In the vignette to chapter 93, to illustrate the protection afforded, a buckle with human hands seizes the arm of the deceased and prevents him from going toward the East, the inauspicious direction for departed souls, pl. xxv (Papyrus, Louvre iii, 93).

[2] Budge, "The Mummy," Cambridge, 1894, p. 259.

eternal youth it was hoped the deceased would enjoy in the realm of the dead. In the 159th chapter of the Book of the Dead, we read of an *uat* of matrix-emerald; it was believed to be the gift of Thoth, serving to protect the limbs of the deceased.[3]

The amulet representing the pillow, *urs*, was generally made of hematite. The 166th chapter of the Book of the Dead is sometimes engraved thereon. Dr. Budge renders this as follows:

> Rise up from non-existence, O prostrate one! They watch over thy head at the exalted horizon. Thou overthrowest thine enemies; thou triumphest over what they do against thee, as Horus, the avenger of his father, this Osiris[4] has commanded to be done for thee. Thou cuttest off the heads of thine enemies; never shall they carry off from thee thy head (?). Verily Osiris maketh slaughter at the coming forth of the heads of his enemies; may they never remove his head from him.

Of all these amulets, the type most frequently encountered has the shape of a heart, *ab*. These are found of carnelian, green jasper, basalt, lapis-lazuli, and other hard materials. The heart, regarded in ancient Egypt as the seat of life, was the object of especial care after death. Enclosed in a special receptacle it was buried with the mummy, and the belief was that only after it had been weighed in the balance of the underworld, against the symbol of law, could it regain its place in the body of the deceased. The heart was symbolically represented by the scarab.[5]

A fine example of a heart amulet shows on one side the figure of the goddess Neith with the pennu bird or

---

[3] Budge, "The Mummy," Cambridge, 1894, p. 261.

[4] The deceased was identified with Osiris.

[5] Budge, "The Mummy," Cambridge, 1894, p. 263.

phœnix, an emblem of the resurrection, and bears inscribed the chapter of the heart.[6]

The following extract from the Book of the Dead treats of the formula to be recited over a funeral scarab cut from a hard stone, perhaps the lapis-lazuli. Egyptian tradition assigned this chapter to the reign of Semti, the fifth king of the 1st Dynasty, about 4400 B.C.[7]

> Chapter of not allowing a man's heart to oppose him in the divine regions of the nether world.
>
> My heart which came from my mother, my heart necessary for my existence on earth, do not rise up against me, do not testify as an adversary against me among the divine chiefs in regard to what I have done before the gods; do not separate from me before the great lord of Amenti. Hail to thee, O heart of Osiris, dwelling in the West! Hail to you, gods of the braided beard, august by your sceptre! Speak well of the Osiris N; make him prosper by Nehbka. I am reunited with the earth, I am not dead in Amenti. There I am a pure spirit for eternity.
>
> To be said over a scarabæus fashioned from a hard stone, coated with gold, and placed on the heart of the man after he has been anointed with oil. The following words should be said over him as a magic charm: "My heart which came from my mother, my heart is necessary for me in my transformations."
>
> Take your aliments, pass around the turquoise basin, and go to him who is in his temple and from whom the gods proceed.

The most ancient inscription of this especially favorite text is on the plinth of a scarab in the British Museum bearing the cartouche of Sebak-em-saf, a king of the XIV Dynasty, 2300 B.C. It is made from an exceptionally fine piece of green jasper, the body and head of the beetle being carefully carved out of the stone, while the legs are of gold, carved in relief. The scarab is inserted into

---

[6] Birch, Catalogue of Egyptian Antiquities in Alnwick Castle, London, 1880, p. 224.

[7] Pierret, "Le livre des Morts," Paris, 1882, p. 138.

"PHANTOM CRYSTAL" OF QUARTZ (ROCK-CRYSTAL) MADAGASCAR.
In possession of the author.

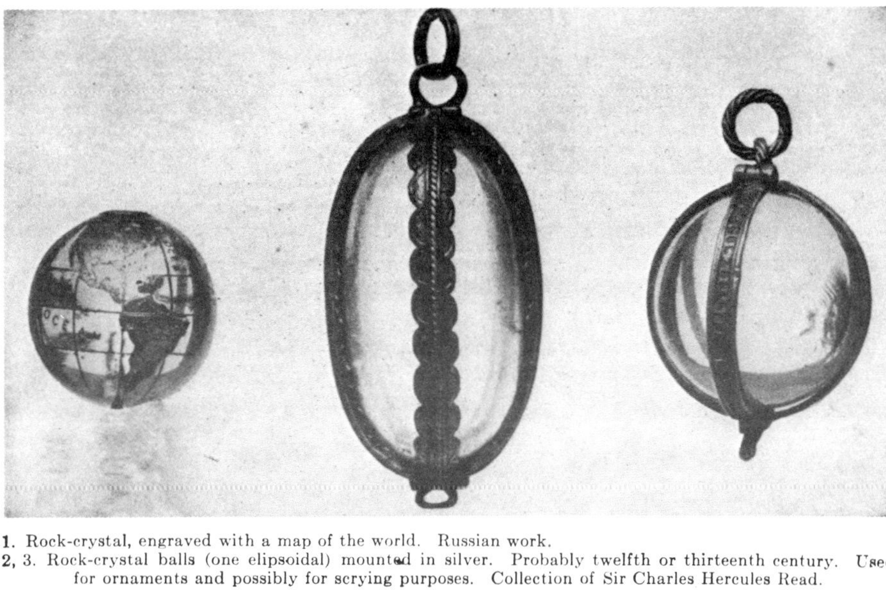

1. Rock-crystal, engraved with a map of the world. Russian work.
2, 3. Rock-crystal balls (one elipsoidal) mounted in silver. Probably twelfth or thirteenth century. Used for ornaments and possibly for scrying purposes. Collection of Sir Charles Hercules Read.

a gold base of tabloid form, and was found at Kurna (Thebes) by Mr. Salt. As green jasper was believed to possess altogether exceptional virtues as an amulet, this particular scarab was probably regarded as especially sacred.

It appears to have been the rule to engrave certain special chapters of the Book of the Dead, among those referring to the heart, upon particular stones. Thus, for instance, the 26th chapter was engraved on lapis-lazuli, the 27th upon feldspar, the 30th upon serpentine, and the 29th upon carnelian.[8] This may perhaps have been originally due to some association of the god principally invoked in the text with the precious substance upon which the text was engraved.

The form of an eye, fashioned out of lapis-lazuli and ornamented with gold, constituted an amulet of great power; it was inscribed with the 140th chapter of the Book of the Dead. On the last day of the month Mechir, an offering "of all things good and holy" was to be made before this symbolic eye, for on that day the supreme god Ra was believed to place such an image upon his head. Sometimes these eyes were made of jasper, and could then be laid upon any of the limbs of a mummy.[9]

Of the image of Truth, made from a lapis-lazuli and worn by the Egyptian high-priest, Ælian aptly says that he would prefer the judge should not bear Truth about with him, fashioned and expressed in an image, but rather in his very soul.[10]

---

[8] "Life Work of Sir Peter le Page Renouf," Paris, 1907, vol. iv, p. 76, note.

[9] Ibid., Paris, 1907, vol. iv, p. 295.

[10] Æliani, "Varia historia," lib. xiv, cap. xxxiv, Lug. Bat., 1731, Pars altera, p. 977.

Among the Assyrian texts giving the formulæ for incantations and various magical operations, there is one which treats of an ornament composed of seven brilliant stones, to be worn on the breast of the king as an amulet; indeed, so great was the virtue of these stones that they were supposed to constitute an ornament for the gods also. The text, as rendered by Fossey, is as follows:[11]

Incantation. The splendid stones! The splendid stones! The stones of abundance and of joy.

Made resplendent for the flesh of the gods.

The *hulalini* stone, the *sirgarru* stone, the *hulalu* stone, the *sându* stone, the *uknû* stone.

The *dushu* stone, the precious stone *elmêshu*, perfect in celestial beauty.

The stone of which the *pingu* is set in gold.

Placed upon the shining breast of the king as an ornament.

Azagsud, high-priest of Bêl, make them shine, make them sparkle!

Let the evil one keep aloof from the dwelling!

The names of two of these gems, the *hulalu* and the *hulalini*, suggest that they were of similar class. As the fundamental meaning of the root whence the names are formed is "to perforate," it is barely possible that we have here the long-sought Assyrian designation for the pearl, which was commonly regarded in ancient times as a stone. In Arabic the perforated pearl has a special name to distinguish it from the unperforated, or "virgin pearl." All we know of the *sându* is that it must have been a dark-colored stone. The *uknû*, however, is almost certainly the lapis-lazuli. It is often mentioned in the Tel el Amarna tablets as having been among the gifts sent by the kings of Babylonia and Assyria to the Pharaohs of Egypt, and also by the latter to friendly Asiatic

[11] Fossey, "La Magie Assyrienne," Paris, 1902, p. 301; see Rawlinson, "Cun. insc. of West. Asia," vol. iv, 18, No. 3.

AMBER HEART-SHAPED AMULET.
Italian, seventeenth century.

AN INSCRIBED SCARAB (GREEN STONE) OF THE TYPE KNOWN AS A HEART-SCARAB. DATE ABOUT 1300 B.C.

The Scribe Pa-bak: Let him say: "O Heart that I received from my mother (to be said twice), O Heart that belongs to my spirit, rise not against me as witness, oppose me not before the judges, contradict me not in the presence of the Guardian of the Scales. Thou art the spirit that is in my body, Khnum that makest sound my limbs. When thou comest to the place of judgment whither we go, cause not my name to be rejected by the assessors, but let the pronouncement of judgment be favorable, and such as causes joy to the heart."

monarchs. Of the *sirgarru* and *dushu* stones nothing is known, but the *elmêshu,* the seventh in the list, was evidently regarded as the most brilliant and splendid of all; indeed, Prof. Friedrich Delitzsch hazards the conjecture that it is the diamond. In any case this stone must have been set in rings and considered very valuable, for in an Assyrian text occurs the following passage: "Like an *elmêshu* ring may I be precious in thine eyes."[12] The fact that this stone is described as having "a celestial beauty" might incline us to believe that it was a sapphire.

The idea of this mystic ornament, composed of seven gems, probably originated in Babylonia, where the number seven was looked upon as especially sacred. As we shall see, there is some reason to attribute a Hindu origin to the nine gems, "the covering" of the King of Tyre, enumerated by Ezekiel, while the breastplate on the ephod of the Hebrew high-priest, with its twelve stones, symbolizing the twelve months of the year, appears to be of later date, and seems to belong to the time of the return from the Babylonian Captivity and the building of the second temple. Certainly, the historic and prophetic books of the Old Testament know nothing of it, although the Urim and Thummim are mentioned and the elaborate description given in Exodus is generally regarded by Biblical scholars as belonging to the so-called "Priestly Codex," the latest part of the Pentateuch, gradually evolved during the Exile and given its final form in the fifth century B.C.

In the very ancient Assyrio-Babylonian epic narrative of the descent of the goddess Ishtar to Hades, the guar-

---

[12] Delitsch, "Assyrisches Wörterbuch," Leipzig, 1896, p. 74, s. v. *elmêshu.*

dian of the infernal regions obliges the goddess to lay aside some part of her clothing and ornaments at each of the seven gates through which she passes. At the fifth, we are told that she stripped off her girdle of *aban alâdi,* or stones which aided parturition.[13] It has been asserted, and perhaps with some reason, that of the many mineral substances supposed to possess this virtue, jade (nephrite) or jadeite was the earliest known.

The Babylonian legends also tell of trees on which grow precious stones. In the Gilgamesh epic a mystic cedar tree is described. This grew in the Elamite sanctuary of Irnina and was under the guardianship of the Elamite king Humbaba. Of this tree an inscription relates:

> It produces *samtu*-stones as fruit;
> Its boughs hang with them, glorious to behold;
> The crown of it produces lapis-lazuli;
> Its fruit is costly to gaze upon.

Another tree bearing precious stones was seen by the hero Gilgamesh, after he had passed through darkness for the space of twelve hours. This must have been a most resplendent object, to judge from the following description on a cuneiform tablet:[14]

> It bore precious stones for fruits;
> Its branches were glorious to the sight;
> The twigs were crystals;
> It bore fruit costly to the sight.

One of the rarest and most significant specimens illustrating the use of valuable stones for religious cere-

---

[13] Jansen, "Assyrisch-Babylonische Mythen und Epen," Berlin, 1900.

[14] Ward, "Seal Cylinders of Western Asia," Carnegie Institution Pub., Washington, D. C., 1910, pp. 232, 234.

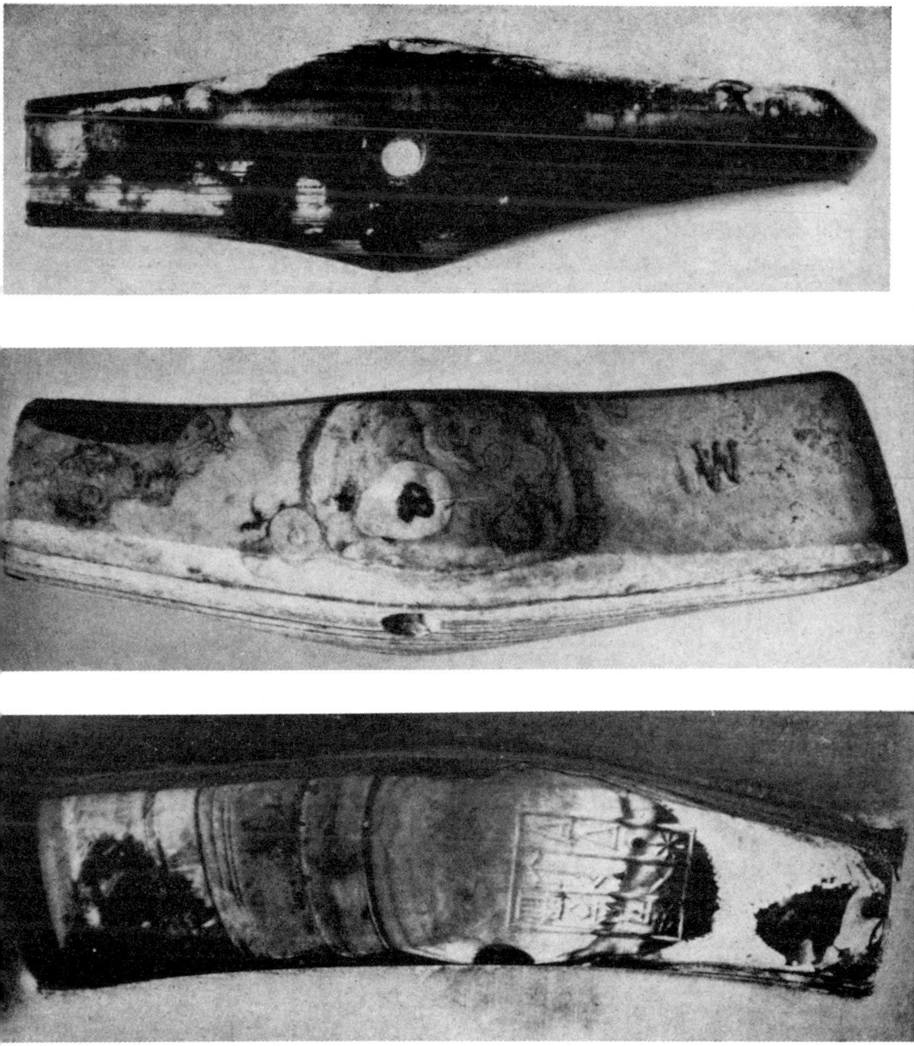

BABYLONIAN AXE HEAD

Agate, with inscription. Morgan collection, American Museum of Natural History, New York.

monial purposes in the pagan world is in the Morgan-Tiffany collection. It is an ancient Babylonian axe-head made of banded agate. So regular, indeed, is the disposition of the layers in this agate that one might be justified in denominating it an onyx. Its prevailing hue is what may be called a "deer-brown"; some white splotches now apparent are evidently due to the action of fire or that of some alkali. This axe-head bears an inscription in archaic cuneiform characters, and presumably in the so-called Sumerian tongue, that believed to have been spoken by the founders of the Babylonian civilization. The form of the inscription indicates that the object dates from an earlier period than 2000 B.C.

While the characters are clearly cut and can be easily deciphered, the inscription is nevertheless exceedingly difficult to translate. It is evident that the axe-head was a votive offering to a divinity, probably on the part of a certain governor named Adduggish; but whether the divinity in question was Shamash (the sun-god), or the god Adad, or some other member of the Babylonian pantheon, cannot be determined with any finality. The French assyriologist, François Lenormant, who first described this axe-head in 1879, and Prof. Ira Maurice Price, of the Semitic Department of Chicago University, both admit that it may have been consecrated to Adad. As the weather-god, the thunderer, the axe-symbol would have been more especially appropriate to him in view of the usage, almost universal among primitive peoples, of associating stone axe-heads or axe-shaped stones with the thunderbolt, and hence with the divinity who was believed to have launched it toward the earth.

This Sumerian axe-head measures 134.5 mm. in length (5.3 inches), 35.5 mm. in width (1.4 inches), and 31 mm. in thickness (1.22 inches). It was originally secured by

Cardinal Stefano Borgia (1731–1804), for some time secretary of the College of the Propaganda in Rome, who probably acquired it from some missionary to the East. From the cardinal's family it passed for 15,000 lire ($3000) to the Tyszkiewicz Collection, and when the objects therein comprised were disposed of at public sale, the writer purchased it for the American Museum of Natural History in New York, April 16, 1902.[15]

At Alicante, in Spain, cut upon the pedestal of an ancient statue, supposed to have been that of Isis, was found an inscription giving a list of the offerings dedicated by divine command, by a certain Fabia Fabiana in honor of her granddaughter. Evidently the fond grandmother had given of her best and choicest jewels which were used to adorn the statue. They consisted of a diadem set with a "unio" (a large round pearl) and six smaller pearls, two emeralds, seven beryls, two rubies, and a hyacinth. In each ear of the statue was inserted an ear-ring bearing a pearl and an emerald; about the neck was hung a necklace consisting of four rows of emeralds and pearls, eighteen of the former and thirty-six of the latter. Two circlets bound around the ankles contained eleven beryls and two emeralds, while two bracelets were set with eight emeralds and eight pearls. The adornment was completed by four rings, two bearing emeralds, while two, placed on the little finger, were set with diamonds. On the sandals were eight beryls.[16]

---

[15] For a fuller description of this valuable relic, and a discussion of the meaning of the inscription, see "On the ancient inscribed Sumerian (Babylonian) axe-head for the Morgan Collection in the American Museum of Natural History," by George Frederick Kunz, with translation by Prof. Ira Maurice Price and discussion by Dr. William Hayes Ward. Bulletin of the Museum, vol. xxi, pp. 37–47, April 6, 1905.

[16] Montfaucon, "L'antiquité expliquée," vol. ii, Pt. II, 1719, pp. 324, 325; Plate 136.

A notable instance of an antique votive offering is the necklace of valuable precious stones dedicated to the statue of Vesta. The Byzantine historian Zosimus attributes the tragic end of Stilicho's widow, Serena, to her having despoiled the image of Vesta of this costly ornament, and finds a sort of poetic justice in the manner of her death, since she was strangled by a cord which encircled her neck.

It is not only in the works of the Fathers of the Christian Church that we find precious stones used as similes of religious virtue, in Buddhist writings also we have examples of this. In the "Questions of King Milinda," composed perhaps as early as the third century of our era, occur the following passages:[17]

> Just, O King, as the diamond is pure throughout; just so, O King, should the strenuous Bhikshu, earnest in effort, be perfectly pure in his means of livelihood. This, O King, is the first quality of the diamond he ought to have.
>
> And again, O King, as the diamond cannot be alloyed with other substance; just so, O King, should the strenuous Bhikshu, earnest in effort, never mix with wicked men as friends. This, O King, is the second quality of the diamond he ought to have.
>
> And again, O King, just as the diamond is set together with the most costly gems; just so, O King, should the strenuous Bhikshu, earnest in effort, associate with those of the highest excellence, with men who have entered the first or second or third stage of the Noble Path, with the jewel treasures of the Arahats, of the recluses of the threefold wisdom, or of the sixfold insight. This, O King, is the third quality of the diamond he ought to have. For it was said, O King, by the Blessed one,[18] the god over all gods, in the Sutta Nipâta:
>
> Let the pure associate with the pure,
> Ever in recollection firm;
> Dwelling harmoniously wise,
> Thus shall ye put an end to griefs.

---

[17] "The Questions of King Milinda," tr. from the Pâli by T. W. Rhys Davids, vol. ii, Oxford, 1894, p. 128.

[18] Buddha.

The description of the New Jerusalem in the book of Revelations finds a curious parallel in the Hindu Puranas. Here we are told that the divine Krishna, the eighth incarnation of Vishnu, took up his abode in the wonderful city Devârakâ, and was visited there by the various orders of gods and geniuses.[19]

> Gods, Asuras, Gandharas, Kinnaras began to pour into Dwáraká, to see Krishna and Valaráma.
>
> Some descended from the sky, some from their cars—and alighting underneath the banyan tree, looked on Dwáraká, the matchless.
>
> The city was square,—it measured a hundred *yojonas,* and over all, was decked in pearls, rubies, diamonds, and other gems.
>
> The city was high,—it was ornamented with gems; and it was furnished with cupolas of rubies and diamonds,—with emerald pillars, and with court-yards of rubies. It contained endless temples. It had cross-roads decked with sapphires, and highways blazing with gems. It blazed like the meridian sun in summer.

As compared with the description in Revelations we cannot fail to note the lack of definiteness. Instead of the well-ordered scheme of color as represented by the twelve precious stones dedicated to the twelve tribes of Israel, the mystic Hindu city is simply a gorgeous mass of the most brilliant gems known in India.

The poetic description of the royal city Kusavati, given in the Maha Sudassana Suttanta, may perhaps have originated in some tradition regarding Ecbatana or Babylon. Seven ramparts surrounded Kusavati, the materials being respectively gold, silver, beryl, crystal, agate, coral and (for the last) "all kinds of gems." In these ramparts were four gates—one of gold, one of silver, one of crystal and one of jade—and at each gate seven pillars were fixed, each three or four times the

---

[19] Surindro Mohun Tagore, "Mani Málá," Pt. II, Calcutta, 1881, pp. 715, 717.

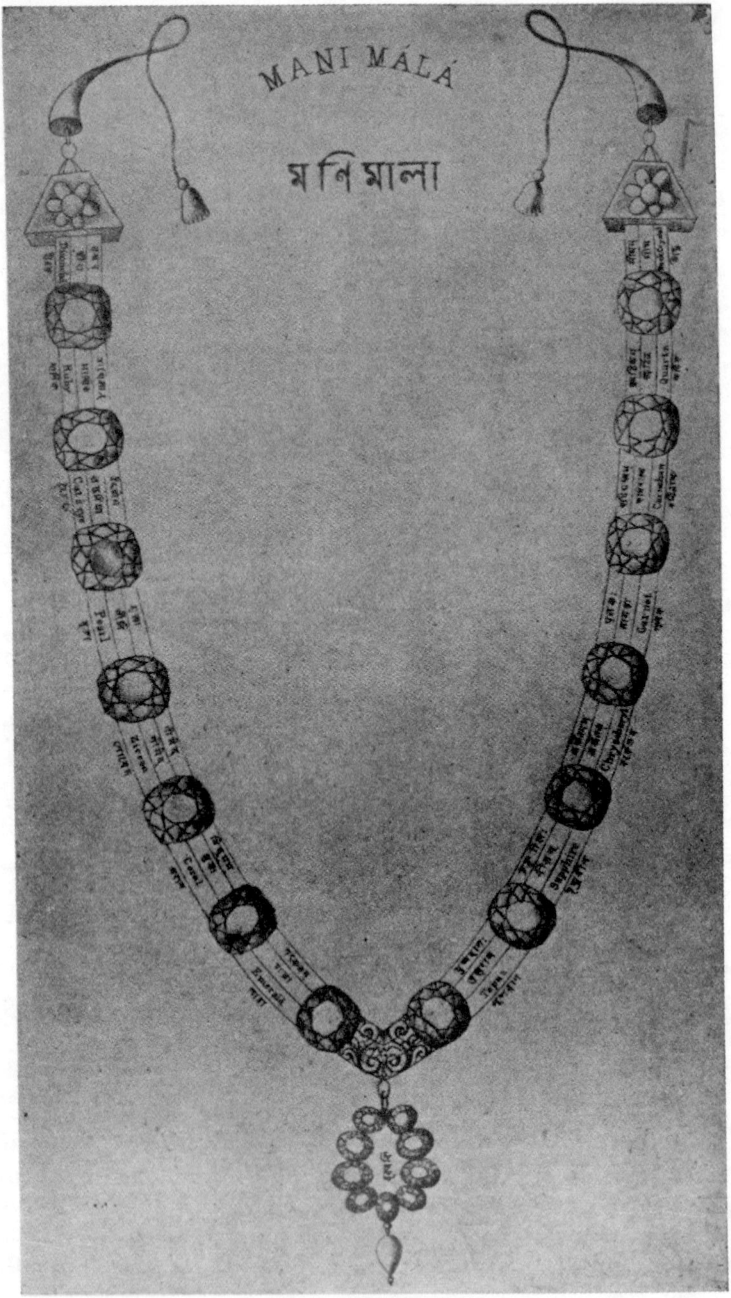

MANI MÁLÁ, OR CHAIN OF GEMS.

Comprising diamond, ruby, cat's-eye, pearl, zircon, coral, emerald, topaz, sapphire, chrysoberyl, garnet, carnelian, quartz and rock-crystal. A pendant is the nao-ratna, or "nine-gem" ornament, suspended from which is a pear-shaped pearl.

In possession of the late Rajah Sir Surindro Mohun Tagore, of Calcutta. From his "Mani Málá," Calcutta, 1879, Vol. I, iv–506 pp., 2 plates, portrait and plate; Vol. II, xiv + ii 507–1046 pp. Contains 49 figures on 10 plates.

height of a man and composed of the seven precious substances that constituted the ramparts. Beyond the ramparts were seven rows of palm trees, the fourth row having trunks of silver and leaves and fruit of gold; then followed palms of beryl, with leaves and fruit of beryl; agate palms, whose fruit and leaves were of coral, and coral palms, with leaves and fruit of agate; lastly, the palms whose trunks were composed of "all kinds of gems," had leaves and fruits of the same description, "and when these rows of palm trees were shaken by the wind, arose a sound sweet and pleasant, and charming and intoxicating."[20]

In Greek literature also there is a "gem-city,"—namely, the city of the Islands of the Blessed, described by Lucian in his Vera Historia.[21] The walls of this city were of emerald, the temples of the gods were formed of beryl, and the altars therein of single amethysts of enormous size. The city itself was all of gold as a fit setting for these marvellous gems.

Hindu mythology tells of a wonderful tank formed of crystal, the work of the god Maya. Its bottom and sides were encrusted with beautiful pearls and in the centre was a raised platform blazing with the most gorgeous precious stones. Although it contained no water, the transparent crystal produced the illusion of water, and those who approached the tank were tempted to plunge into it and take a refreshing bath in what appeared to be clear, fresh water.[22]

---

[20] Bhuddist Suttas, trans. from Pali by T. W. Rhys Davids; "Sacred Books of the East," vol. xi, Oxford, 1881.

[21] Lib. ii, cap. 11. Luciani Opera, ex recog. C. Jacobitz, vol. i, Leipzig, 1884, p. 56.

[22] Surindro Mohun Tagore, "Mani Málá," Pt. II, Calcutta, 1881, p. 79.

The Kalpa Tree of Hindu religion, a symbolical offering to the gods, is described by Hindu poets as a glowing mass of precious stones. Pearls hung from its boughs and beautiful emeralds from its shoots; the tender young leaves were corals, and the ripe fruit consisted of rubies. The roots were of sapphire; the base of the trunk of diamond, the uppermost part of cat's-eye, while the section between was of topaz. The foliage (except the young leaves) was entirely formed of zircons.[23]

The Chinese Buddhist pilgrim Heuen Tsang, who visited India between 629 and 645 A.D., tells of the wonderful "Diamond Throne" which, according to the legend, had once stood near the Tree of Knowledge, beneath whose spreading branches Gautama Buddha is said to have received his supreme revelation of truth. This throne had been constructed in the age called the "Kalpa of the Sages"; its origin was contemporaneous with that of the earth, and its foundations were at the centre of all things; it measured one hundred feet in circumference, and was made of a single diamond. When the whole earth was convulsed by storm or earthquake this resplendent throne remained immovable. Upon it the thousand Buddhas of the Kalpa had reposed and had fallen into the "ecstasy of the diamond." However, since the world has passed into the present and last age, sand and earth have completely covered the "Diamond Throne," so that it can no longer be seen by human eye.[24]

In the Kalpa Sutra, written in Prakrit, one of the sacred books of the Jains, the rivals of the Buddhists, it is said that Harinegamesi, the divine commander of the

---

[23] Surindro Mohun Tagore, "Mani Málá," Pt. II, Calcutta, 1881, pp. 645, 647.

[24] Heuen Tsang, "Mémoires sur les contrées occidentales," French trans. by Stanislas Julien, Paris, 1857, vol. i, p. 461.

foot troops, seized fourteen precious stones, the chief of which was *vajra,* the diamond, and rejecting their grosser particles, retained only the finer essence to aid him in his transformations. In the same sutra the following glowing description is given of the adornment of the surpassingly beautiful goddess Sri:[25]

> On all parts of her body shone ornaments and trinkets, composed of many jewels and precious stones, yellow and red gold. The pure cup-like pair of her breasts sparkled, encircled by a garland of Kunda flowers in which glittered a string of pearls. She wore strings of pearls made by clever and diligent artists, strung with wonderful strings, a necklace of jewels with a string of Dinaras, and a trembling pair of earrings, touching her shoulders, diffused a brilliancy; but the united beauties and charms of these ornaments were only subservient to the loveliness of her face.

As engraved decoration of a fine Chinese vase of white jade with delicate crown markings, appear eight storks, each of which bears in its beak an attribute of one of the Eight Taoist Immortals. Thus we have the double gourd as attribute of the most powerful of these demi-gods known as "Li with the Iron Crutch," whose aid is sought by magicians and astrologers; the magic sword, with which Lu T'ung-pin vanquished the spirits of evil that roamed through the Chinese Empire in the form of terrible dragons; the basket of flowers, attribute of Lan Ts'ai-ho, the patron of gardeners and florists; the royal fan used by Han Chung-li, of the Chow Dynasty (1122-220 B.C.), to call again to life the spirits of the departed; the lotus flower, emblematic of the virgin Ho Hsien-Ku, venerated somewhat as a patron saint by Chinese housewives, and who acquired the gift of immortal life by the help of a powder of pulverized jade and mother-of-pearl;

[25] Gaina Sutras, trans. from Prakrit by Hermann Jacobi; "Sacred Books of the East," vol.xxii, Oxford, 1884, pp. 227, 233.

the bamboo tubes and rods with which the mighty necromancer Chang Kuo, patron of artists, evoked the souls of the dead; the flute of the musicians' patron, Han Hsiang-tzu, who owed his immortality to his craft in stealthily entering the Taoist paradise and securing a peach from the sacred tree of life; and, lastly, the castanets of Tsao Kuo-chin, especially revered by Chinese actors.

The prevailing belief in India, that treasures offered to the images or shrines of the gods will bring good fortune to the generous donor, finds expression in many ancient and modern Hindu writings. In the Rig Veda it is said that "by giving gold the giver receives a life of light and glory." In the Samaveda Upanishad we read: "Givers are high in Heaven. Those who give horses live conjointly with the sun; givers of gold enjoy eternal life; givers of clothes live in the moon." Another text (Hâiti Smriti) reads:[26]

> Coral in worship will subdue all the three worlds. He who worships Krishna with rubies will be reborn as a powerful emperor; if with a small ruby, he will be born a king. Offering emeralds will produce Gyana or Knowledge of the Soul and of the Eternal. If he worships with a diamond, even the impossible, or Nirvâna, that is Eternal Life in the highest Heaven, will be secured. If with a flower of gold a man worships for a month, he will get as much wealth as Kuvera, the Lord of Rubies, and will hereafter attain to Nirvâna and to Muskwa, or Salvation.

At Multan, one of the most ancient cities of India, situated in the Punjab, 164 miles southwest of Lahore, there was in the Hindu temple an idol having for eyes two great pearls. The eyes of the rude image of Jagganath at Puri, in Bengal (Orissa), are said to have

[26] Hendley, "Indian Jewellery," London, 1909, p. 33.

at one time been formed of precious stones, as were also those of the idols of Vishnu at Chandernagore and in the great seven-walled temple at Srirangam, whence appears to have come the Orloff diamond.

In ceremonial worship the Hindus recognize sixteen offerings, the ninth consisting of gems and jewelry, and a divine assurance of adequate return to the giver appears in the Bhagavat Purana, where Krishna says, "Whatever is best and most valued in this world and that which is most dear to you should be offered to me, and it will be received back in immense and endless quantity." On certain appointed days the holy images are decorated with the choicest garments and the richest jewelry in the temple treasury; this is especially the case on the day celebrated as the birthday of the respective divinity. However, the gifts are believed to retain their sacred character as dedicated objects only for a comparatively brief period, varying from a month or more for garments and vestments, to ten or twelve years for jewels, such as the naoratna or the panchratna, the prized and revered jewels, composed respectively of nine and five gems. The panchratna usually consists of gold, diamond, sapphire, ruby, and pearl. After the gifts have ceased to be worthy of use in the temples, they may be disposed of to defray the expenses of the foundation, including the cost of supporting the numerous priests and attendants. As the objects still retain their sacred associations, they are eagerly bought by pious Hindus, who undoubtedly regard them as valuable talismans. Thus they not only serve to bring blessings upon the donors, but also constitute one of the chief sources of income for the temples.[27]

---

[27] Hendley, "Indian Jewellery," London, 1909, pp. 33, 34.

One of the oldest and perhaps the most interesting talismanic jewel is that known as the naoratna or nararatna, the "nine-gem" jewel. It is mentioned in the old Hindu ratnaçastras, or treatises on gems, for example, in the Nararatnaparîkshâ, where it is described as follows:[28]

Manner of composing the setting of a ring:

In the centre	The Sun	The Ruby
To the East	Venus	The Diamond
To the Southeast	The Moon	The Pearl
To the South	Mars	The Coral
To the Southwest	Râhu	The Jacinth
To the West	Saturn	The Sapphire
To the Northeast	Jupiter	The Topaz
To the North	The descending node	The Cat's-eye
To the Northwest	Mercury	The Emerald

Such is the planetary setting.

From this description we learn that the jewel was designed to combine all the powerful astrological influences. The gems chosen to correspond with the various heavenly bodies, and with the aspects known as the ascending and descending nodes, differ in some cases from those selected in the West. For instance, the emerald is here assigned to Mercury, whereas in Western tradition this stone was usually the representative of Venus, although it is sometimes associated with Mercury also.[29] On the other hand, the diamond is dedicated to Venus, instead of to the Sun as in the Western world.

In the naoratna the five gems known to the Hindus as the mahâratnâni, or "great gems,"—the diamond, pearl,

---

[28] Finot, "Les lapidaries indiens," Paris, 1896, p. 175.

[29] Morales, "De las piedras preciosas," Valladolid, 1604 (fol. 16 verso).

ruby, sapphire, and emerald,—were, as we see, associated with the Sun and Moon, Venus, Mercury, and Saturn, while the four lesser gems (uparatnâni)—namely, the jacinth, topaz, cat's-eye, and coral—represent Mars, Jupiter, Râhu, and the descending node. The two last named are very important factors in astrological calculations and are often called the Dragon's Head and the Dragon's Tail. These designations signify the ascending and descending nodes, indicating the passage of the ecliptic by the Moon in her ascent above and descent below this arbitrary plane.

In three somewhat obscure passages of the Rig Veda there are references to the seven ratnas. Whether these were gems cannot be determined, since the primary meaning of the word ratna is "a precious object," not necessarily a precious stone; but it is possible that we may have here an allusion to some earlier form of talisman, in which only the Sun, Moon, and the five planets were represented.

It is easy to understand that such a talisman as the naoratna, combining the favorable influences of all the celestial bodies supposed to govern the destinies of man, must have been highly prized, and we may well assume that only the rich and powerful could own this talisman in a form ensuring its greatest efficacy. For the Hindus believed that the virtue of every gem depended upon its perfection, and they regarded a poor or defective stone as a source of unhappiness and misfortune.

In modern times this talisman is sometimes differently composed. A specimen shown in the Indian Court of the Paris Exposition of 1878 consisted of the following stones: coral, topaz, sapphire, ruby, flat diamond, cut diamond, emerald, amethyst, and carbuncle. Here the cut diamond, amethyst, and carbuncle take the place of the jacinth, pearl, and cat's-eye.

Instead of uniting the different planetary gems in a single ring, they have sometimes been set separately in a series of rings to be worn successively on the days originally named after the celestial bodies. We read in the life of Apollonius of Tyana (first century A.D.) by Philostratus: "Damis also relates that Iarchas gave to Apollonius seven rings named after the planets, and the latter wore these, one by one, in the order of the weekdays."[30] Although it is not expressly stated that the appropriate stones were set in the rings, the custom of the time makes it probable that this was the case.

NINE GEMS.

English	Sanskrit	Burmese	Chinese (Canton)	Arabic
Diamond	Vajra	Chein	Chun-syak	Mâs
Ruby	Manikya	Budmiya	Se-fla-yu-syak	Yâkût bihar
Cat's-eye	Vaidûrya	Châno	Mâu-ji gan	Ain al-hirr
Zircon	Gomeda	Gomok	Pi-si	Hajar yamânî
Pearl	Muktâ	Pa-le	Chun-ti	Lûlû
Coral	Pravâla	Tadâ	Sau-ho-chi	Murjân
Emerald	Marakata	Mujâ	Luk-syak	Zumurrud
Topaz	Pushyaraga	Outfiyâ	Si-lang-syak	Yâkût al-azrak
Sapphire	Nîla	Nîlâ	Chang-syak	Yâkût al-açfar

Among the Burmese the value for occult purposes of the nine gems composing the naoratna, or nararatna, is strictly determined in the following order: first, the ruby; second, the diamond, or rock-crystal; third, the pearl; fourth, the coral; fifth, the topaz; sixth, the sapphire; seventh, the cat's-eye; eighth, the amethyst; and ninth, the emerald.[31] That the ruby, diamond and pearl should occupy places of honor is quite natural, but the rele-

[30] Philostrati, "De Vita Apollonii," lib. iii, cap. 36.

[31] Personal communication from Taw Sein Ko.

SCULPTURED JADE MOUNTAIN.

Probably the largest mass of sculptured jade in existence. The design commemorates the meetings of a literary club of the fourth century. The Chinese characters (colored red) in the side of the cliff express the famous *Lan Ting Hsu*, or "Epidendron Pavilion Essay," by Wang Hi-che (A.D. 321–379), ever since used by the Chinese as a model of elegant caligraphy, and were engraved directly from the autograph of the Emperor Ch'ien-lung, written by him in 1784. Height 23 inches, width 38½ x 18½ inches; weight 640 pounds. From the Summer Palace, west of Peking. Collection of T. D. Walker, of Minneapolis, Minn.

gation of the sapphire to sixth place, after coral and topaz, seems to be a rather unfair treatment of this beautiful stone.

The yellow girdles worn by the Chinese emperors of the Manchu dynasty were variously ornamented with precious stones according to the different ceremonial observances at which the emperor presided. For the services in the Temple of Heaven, the very appropriate choice of lapis-lazuli ornaments was made; for the Altar of Earth, yellow jade was favored; for a sacrifice on the Altar of the Sun, the gems were red corals, while white jade was selected for the ceremonies before the Altar of the Moon. Jade of different colors was used for the six precious tablets employed in the worship of heaven and earth and the four cardinal points. For the worship of Heaven there was the dark-green round tablet; for that of Earth, an octagonal tablet of yellow jade. The East was worshipped with a green pointed tablet; the West was worshipped with the white "tiger-tablet"; the North with a black, semi-circular tablet, and the South with a tablet of red jade.[32]

Of all the Chinese works on jade the most interesting and remarkable is the *Ku yü t'ou pu* or "Illustrated Description of Ancient Jade," a catalogue divided into a hundred books and embellished with upward of seven hundred figures. It was published in 1176, and lists the magnificent collection of jade objects belonging to the first emperor of the Southern Sung dynasty. One of the treasures here described was a four-sided plaque of pure white jade over two feet in height and breadth, and it was

---

[32] The Bishop Collection: "Investigations and Studies in Jade," New York, 1906, vol. i, p. 54, The "Yushuo" of T'ang Jing-tso, trans. by Stephen W. Bushnell.

regarded as of altogether exceptional value, for on it was a design miraculously engraven. This was a figure, seated on a mat, with a flower-vase on its left and an alms-bowl on the right, in the midst of rocks enveloped in clouds. The figure was an image of the Buddhist saint, Samantabahadra, and the plaque is said to have been washed out of a sacred cave in the year 1068, by a violent and mysterious current.[33]

Jade talismans are very popular at the present day in the Mohammedan world, and among the Turks they are so highly prized as heirlooms that it is difficult to secure any of them. There is an orthodox Mohammedan sect, whose members call themselves Pekdash, and who during their whole lifetime carry about with them a flat piece of jade as a protection against injury or annoyance of every kind.[34]

The four rain-making gods are shown wearing necklaces of coral and turquoise in the ceremonial sand-paintings of the Navajos. These four gods are respectively colored to denote the four cardinal points; black for North, blue for South, yellow for West, and white for East. The whole painting, measuring nine by thirteen feet, is guarded on three sides by magic wands; toward the East it is left unprotected, as only good spirits are believed to dwell in this direction. Each of the rain-gods carries suspended from his right wrist an elaborately decorated tobacco pouch, bearing the figure of a stone pipe. The Navajos believe that in this pouch the god places a ray of sunlight with which he lights his pipe;

---

[33] The Bishop Collection: "Investigations and Studies in Jade," New York, 1906, vol. i, p. 36.

[34] Kobert, "Ein Edelstein der Vorzeit," Stuttgart, 1910, p. 26.

when he smokes, clouds form in the sky and the rain descends. In the sand-picture representing the God of the Whirlwind this divinity also wears ear-pendants and a necklace of turquoise.[35]

Of the turquoise in Aztec times we have the testimony of the missionary Bernardino de Sahagun that one variety, presumably that regarded as the finest and most attractive, bore the name *teuxivitl,* which signified "turquoise of the gods." No one was allowed either to own or wear this as it was exclusively devoted to the service of the gods, whether as a temple offering, or for the decoration of the divine images. Sahagun describes this turquoise as "fine, unspotted and very clear. It was very rare and was brought to Mexico from afar. Some specimens were of rounded shape, like a hazel-nut cut in half; others were broad and flat, and some were pitted as though in a state of decomposition."[36]

The god of fire, Xiuhtecutli, or Ixçocauhqui, presided over the ceremony of piercing the ears of the young boys and girls. The image of this god was decorated with ear-rings encrusted with a mosaic of turquoise. He held in his left hand a buckler on which were five large green stones called *chalchiuitl* (jadeite), placed in the form of a cross on a plate of gold almost covering the shield.[37]

At the time of the Spanish Conquest an immense emerald, almost as large as an ostrich egg, was adored by the Peruvians in the city of Manta. This "emerald goddess" bore the name of Umiña, and, like some of

[35] Alfred Marston Tozzer, "Navajo Religious Ceremonials," Putnam Anniversary Volume, New York, 1909, pp. 323–326, 329, Plate II.

[36] Sahagun, "Historia general de las cosas de Nueva España," Mexico, 1830, vol. iii, p. 297.

[37] Sahagun, l. c., 1829, vol. i, p. 18; lib. i, cap. xiii.

the precious relics of the Christian world, was only exhibited on high feast days, when the Indians flocked to the shrine from far and near, bringing gifts to the goddess. The wily priests especially recommended the donation of emeralds, saying that these were the daughters of the goddess, who would be well pleased to see her offspring. In this way an immense store of emeralds rewarded the efforts of the priests, and on the conquest of Peru all these fine stones fell into the hands of Pedro de Alvarado,[38] Garcilasso de la Vega, and their companions. The mother emerald, however, had been so cleverly concealed by the priests of the shrine that the Spaniards never succeeded in gaining possession of it. Many of the other emeralds were destroyed because of the ignorance and stupidity of some of their new owners, who, supposing that the test of a true emerald was its ability to withstand hard blows, laid the stones on an anvil and hammered them to pieces. The old and entirely false notion that the genuine diamond could endure this treatment may have suggested the unfortunate test.

Garcilasso likens the growth of the emerald in its mine to that of a fruit on a tree, and he believed that it gradually acquired its beautiful green hue, that part of the crystal nearest the sun being the first to acquire color. He notes an interesting specimen found in Peru, half of which was colorless like glass, while the other half was a brilliant green; this he compares with a half-ripened fruit.[39]

The remarkable jade adze, generally known as the

---

[38] Garcilasso de la Vega, "Histoire des Incas." Fr. trans. by Jean Baudoin, Amsterdam, 1715, vol. ii, pp. 255–257.

[39] Ibid., p. 347.

"Kunz adze," was found in Oaxaca, Mexico, brought to the United States about 1890, and is now in the American Museum of Natural History, New York. Of a light greenish-gray hue, with a slight tinge of blue, this jade artefact is 272 mm. long ($10^{13}/_{16}$ inches), 153 mm. wide (6 inches) and 118 mm. thick ($4\frac{5}{8}$ inches); its weight is 229.3 Troy ounces, nearly sixteen pounds avoirdupois. Rudely, but not unskilfully, carved upon its face is a grotesque human figure. Four small, shallow depressions, one under each eye and one near each hand, may have served to hold in place small gold films, but no trace of gold decoration is now extant. In its mechanical execution this adze offers evidence of considerable skill on the part of the Aztec lapidary, the polish equalling that of modern workers. In the fact that a large piece, which must apparently have weighed at least two pounds, has evidently been cut out of this implement by some one of its Indian owners, we can see a proof of the talismanic power ascribed to jadeite in Aztec times, for there can be little doubt that nothing less than a belief in the great virtue of jadeite coupled with the rarity of the material could have induced the mutilation of what must have been regarded in its time as a remarkable work of art.[40]

The source of the prehistoric jade (nephrite and jadeite) found in Europe, and also of that worked into ornaments by the Indians before the Spanish Conquest of America, was long the subject of contention among mineralogists and archæologists. In Germany this question was denominated the *Nephritfrage,* and the most notable contribution to the discussion was the great scien-

[40] "A Remarkable Jadeite Adze," American Association for the Advancement of Science. Kunz, "Gems and Precious Stones of North America," New York, 1890, pp. 278–280.

tific and scholarly work issued by Heinrich Fischer.[41] His conclusion was that as there was no evidence of the existence of these minerals outside of a few localities in Asia, the European and American supply must have been brought to these parts of the world from Asia, and that hence the presence of these jade artefacts in America clearly pointed to commercial intercourse at an early period between the American continent and Asia, and might be regarded as offering a strong argument in favor of an Asiatic origin for an American civilization. According to this theory the prehistoric jade objects found in Europe must have had a similar source, and would constitute a proof of the existence of traffic with remote points in Asia at a date long previous to that commonly accepted.

This view was strongly opposed by Prof. A. B. Meyer, of Dresden, and recent discoveries have effectively disproved the theory in the case of Europe at least, for nephrite has been found there *in situ* in several places. The largest mass of this material that has been taken from a European deposit is that found by the writer at Jordansmühl in Silesia, in April, 1899, and which weighed 4704 pounds.[42] The origin of American jade in the forms of nephrite and jadeite has not yet been definitely determined, but we have every reason to suppose that deposits of these minerals will eventually be discovered in various parts of the American continent, as they have already

---

[41] "Nephrit und Jadite," Stuttgart, 1880.

[42] The Bishop Collection, "Investigations and Studies in Jade," New York, 1906, vol. i, pt. iii, "Jade as a Mineral," by George Frederick Kunz, p. 177. This immense mass of nephrite which forms part of the Heber Bishop Collection loan of jade is now in the American Museum of Natural History, New York.

been in Europe. Indeed, the existence of nephrite in Alaska is already well attested.

The peculiar and characteristic qualities of these substances have made them favorite materials for ornamental objects from the earliest ages down to our own day, and in almost all parts of the world. A most important element contributing to the popularity of jade has been its supposed possession of wonderful talismanic and therapeutic virtues, and while the Western world has not the same belief in these matters as the Eastern world, a more or less definite appreciation of what jade still signifies for many in the Orient, continues to exercise an influence over both Americans and Europeans, making objects of nephrite or jadeite highly prized everywhere at the present time.

The term *chalchihuitl* was indifferently applied by the ancient Mexicans to a number of green or greenish-white stones; *quetzal chalchihuitl,* which was regarded as the most precious variety, may perhaps have more exclusively denoted jadeite. This is somewhat indefinitely described by Sahagun as being "white, with much transparency, and with a slight greenish tinge, something like jasper." Of eight ornamental objects of green stone examined some years ago by the writer, four were of jadeite, one of serpentine, another of green quartz, and the remaining two of a mixture of white feldspar and green hornblende. An inferior kind of *chalchihuitl,* said by Sahagun to have come from quarries in the vicinity of Tecalco, appears to have been identical with the so-called "Mexican onyx" which is found in veins in that place and is an aragonite stalagmite. This material, from which figures, ornaments and beads were made by the ancient Mexicans, is to-day greatly valued as an ornamental stone.

The greater number of ancient Mexican jadeite beads appear to have been rounded pebbles of this material, assorted as to size and drilled for use in making necklaces. Other green stones used at this time in Mexico were green jasper, green plasma, serpentine and also the "Tecalco onyx" or "marble" above mentioned. In many cases these substances are of such rich green that they might easily be mistaken for jadeite by those who lacked the tests or the experience at the command of modern mineralogists. Should jadeite ever be found *in situ* in Mexico, it seems probable that the discovery will be made in the State of Oaxaca, whence came the finest ancient specimens, including the splendid votive adze. Moreover, one of the few materials by which jadeite can be worked is furnished by the streams of this region, whence have been taken several rolled pebbles which the writer has identified as yellow and blue corundum, the quality being equal to that of specimens from Ceylon.[43]

Gesner describes one of the lip ornaments worn by the aborigines of South America in the following words: [44]

> A green stone or gem which the inhabitants of the West Indies use. They pierce their lips and insert this stone so that the thicker part adheres to the hole and the rest protrudes. We might call these ornaments *oripenduli* [mouth-pendants]. This stone was given me by a learned Piedmontese, Johannes Ferrerius, and he wrote of it as follows: "I send a cylindrical green stone, as long as a man's middle finger, and having at one extremity two ridges. It is stated that the Brazilians of high rank wore these, from their youth, in their pierced lips; one or more being worn according to the dignity of the wearer. While eating, or whenever they so wish for any other reason, these ornaments are removed from the lips."

[43] Kunz, "Chalchiuitl: a note on the jadeite discussion," Science, vol. xii, No. 298.

[44] Gesneri, "De figuris lapidum," Tiguri, 1565, fol. 107 verso, 108 recto.

VOTIVE ADZE OF JADEITE FROM MEXICO.

a. Front view. b. Side view. c. Rear view. Kunz Collection, American Museum of Natural History, New York. $10\frac{13}{16}$ x 6 x $4\frac{5}{8}$ inches.

Similar ornaments, made of a green quartz and of beryl, are in the Kunz collection in the Field Museum of Chicago.

The reason for these strange mutilations, which often cause serious discomfort to those who practice them, is not at all easy to determine. Some have conjectured that by the insertion of bright, colored objects in the ears, nose and lips, members of the same tribe were enabled to recognize each other at a distance; each tribe having selected a particular color. However, although certain local preferences are shown in the matter of color or material, there is no hard and fast rule in this matter, and frequently neighboring tribes will employ stones or shells of the same or similar hue and appearance. Others find in this custom a religious significance and suppose that the mutilation represents a form of sacrifice to the spirits, good or bad, who must be rendered favorable to man by some act on his part showing his unconditional submission to them. Originating in this way the idea of adornment was a secondary impulse. It is a fact that ancient peoples regarded the wearing of ear-rings as a badge of slavery, and, according to a Rabbinical legend, Eve's ears were pierced as a punishment for her disobedience, when she was driven from the Garden of Eden.

A curious theory was advanced by Knopf.[45] He calls attention to the habit children have of thrusting small bright objects into their noses and ears, and suggests that this indicates a natural propensity which, coupled with the early-developed love of adornment, induced primitive man to affix ornamental objects on or in the nose, ear, or mouth. There may be more in this than we are willing to admit, but on the whole it seems

[45] "De ornatu oris, nasi et aurium," Gottingæ, 1832, p. 43.

most probable that ceremonial and religious considerations gave rise to the custom.

One of the largest masses of sculptured Chinese jade is in the collection of T. B. Walker, Esq., of Minneapolis. This shows a jade mountain, with groups of figures artistically placed at its base, and winding pathways up to its summit. On the face of the rock is inscribed in beautiful Chinese characters the Epidendron Pavilion Essay of Wang Hi-che, a masterpiece of Chinese calligraphy.

An enormous mass of New Zealand jade (punamu, "green stone") weighing 7000 pounds, found in South Island in 1902, is to be seen in the Museum of Natural History, New York; it was secured by the writer and was donated to the Museum by the late J. Pierpont Morgan. This is the largest mass of jade known, or of which we have any record. On it is placed a remarkable and, in its own peculiar way, an artistic decoration, serving as a type of old Maori life, and at the same time designating the geographic source of the jade in a striking and unmistakable manner calculated to appeal to the least intelligent visitor. This is a statue of a Maori warrior of the old days, executing a war dance, characteristics of which were a distortion of the features and a thrusting out of the tongue intended to express defiance and contempt of the enemy; the time or cadence of the dance was marked by slapping the thigh with the flat of the left hand. This figure was executed from life by Sigurd Neandross; indeed it was actually cast from the model, so that there can be no doubt as to its fidelity.

Rock-crystal is included among the various objects used as fetiches by the Cherokee Indians. This stone is believed to have great power to give aid in hunting and also in divining. One owner of such a crystal kept his magic stone wrapped up in buckskin and hid it in a sacred cave; at stated intervals he would take it out of its repository and "feed" it by rubbing over it the blood of a deer. This goes to prove that the stone, as a fetich, was considered to be a living entity and as such to require nourishment.[46]

Precious stones have been everywhere regarded as especially appropriate offerings at the shrine of a divinity, for the worshipper naturally thought that what was most valuable and beautiful in his eyes must also be most pleasing to the divinity he worshipped. However, we rarely find the usage which was remarked by Francisco Lopez de Gomara among the Indians of New Granada about the time of the Spanish Conquest.[47] These natives "burned gold and emeralds" before the images of the sun and moon, which were regarded as the highest divinities. Certainly to use precious stones for a "burnt offering" was an original and curious idea, although we have abundant proof that pearls were offered in this way by the mound-builders of the Mississippi Valley. In this case great quantities of pearls were burned at the obsequies of the chiefs of the tribes, or at those of any one belonging to the family of a chief.

In ancient Mexico the lapidaries adored the four following divinities as their tutelary gods: Chiconaui Itzcuintli ("nine dogs"), Naualpilli ("noble necromancer"), Macuilcalli ("five horses"), and Cintectl ("the god of harvest"). A festival was celebrated in honor of the three last-named divinities when the zodiacal sign called *chiconaui itzcuintli* was in the ascendant. A feminine divinity represented this sign and to her was attributed the invention of the garments and the orna-

---

[46] "Handbook of American Indians North of Mexico," ed. by Frederick Webb Hodge; Smithsonian Inst., Bur. of Am. Ethn. Bull. 30. Pt. I, p. 458; Washington, 1910.

[47] "Historia de las Indias," in "Bib. de autores españoles," vol. xxii, Madrid, 1852, p. 202.

ments worn by women. The four gods of the lapidaries were looked upon as the discoverers and teachers of the art of cutting precious stones and of piercing and polishing them, as well as of the making of labrets and earflaps of obsidian, rock-crystal, or amber. They also were the inventors of necklaces and bracelets.[48]

The stones worn by Chinese mandarins as a designation of their rank were undoubtedly determined originally by religious or ceremonial considerations. They are as follows; it will be noticed that red stones are given the preference:

Red or pink tourmaline, ruby (and rubellite)........	1st rank.
Coral or an inferior red stone (garnet)	2d rank.
Blue stone (beryl or lapis-lazuli)..................	3d rank.
Rock-crystal	4th rank.
Other white stones	5th rank.

The knowledge of classical mythology was so slight among the ecclesiastics of the Middle Ages that some very queer attributions of the subjects engraved on Greek and Roman gems were made during this period. A reliquary containing a tooth of the Apostle Peter, preserved in the Cathedral of Troyes, was set with antique gems which had been plundered by French and Venetian crusaders from the treasure-house of the Greek Emperor in Constantinople, when that city was sacked in 1204 during the Fourth Crusade. Among these gems was one representing Leda and the Swan—certainly a curious subject for the adornment of a Christian reliquary. Another Greek or Roman gem, long preserved in a church, was furnished by its Christian owners with an inscription

[48] Sahagun, "Historia general de las cosas de Nueva España," Mexico, 1829, vol. ii, pp. 389–391, lib. ix, cap. xvii.

indicating that the figure engraved upon it was that of St. Michael, while in reality it was a representation of the god Mercury. Still another gem was provided with an inscription signifying that the subject was the temptation of Mother Eve in the Garden of Eden, but the Greek gem engraver's intent had been to carve the figures of Zeus and Athena, standing before an olive tree, a design which appears on some Athenian coins; at the feet of the divinities appears a serpent. In a similar way the grain-measure crowning the head of Jupiter-Serapis led to the attribution of a gem so engraved to the patriarch Joseph.[49]

An engraved amethyst bearing the figure of a little Cupid is said to have been worn in a ring by St. Valentine. While this may be somewhat doubtful, it is by no means impossible, for many pagan gems were worn by pious Christians, who reconciled their consciences to the use of these beautiful but scarcely religious ornaments by giving to the pagan symbols a Christian meaning. Certainly, in view of the time-honored customs connected with St. Valentine's Day, there seems something peculiarly appropriate in the design of the ring supposed to have been worn by St. Valentine.

That precious stones had sense and feeling was quite generally believed in medieval times, and a legend told of St. Martial illustrates this idea. The gloves worn by this saint were studded with precious stones, and when on a certain occasion a sacrilegious act was committed in his presence, the gems, horrified at the sight, sprang out of their settings and fell to the ground before the eyes of the onlookers.

---

[49] Klot, "Ueber den Nützen und Gebrauch der alten geschnittenen Steine," Altenburg, 1768, p. 57.

The St. Sylvester or St. James stone is a banded agate in two colors, the one dark and the other light, with a cat's-eye effect so that both colors are equally visible. The light side represents the old year, with its known occurrences, and the opaque side represents the new year, which is dark like futurity. This is a typical stone for a New Year's present or for one born on St. Sylvester's Day, the last day of the year. The popular tradition is that the member of a family or a household who is last to arise on that day will be the last to arise all the year around.

DE OMNI RERVM FOSSILIVM GENERE, GEMMIS, LAPIDIBVS, METALLIS, ET HVIVSMODI, LIBRI ALIQVOT, PLERIQVE NVNC PRIMVM EDITI.

Opera Conradi Gesneri: Quorum Catalogum sequens folium continet.

Tiguri, excudebat Iacobus Gesnerus. Anno M. D. LXV.

TITLE PAGE OF A GROUP OF TREATISES BY VARIOUS AUTHORS, COLLECTED AND EDITED BY CONRAD GESNER AT ZÜRICH IN 1565.

The upper one of the two rings figured is set with a natural pointed diamond, the lower one with a piece of amber enclosing an insect; grouped around are twelve stones representing those of the Breastplate.

The famous "Sacro Catino" preserved in Genoa was long believed to be made of a single immense emerald, but careful investigation proved that it was of no more valuable material than green glass. A legend still current in the early part of the sixteenth century represented this cup, or dish, as having been used by Christ at the Last Supper, and stated that it was one of the utensils which King Herod ordered to be brought from Galilee to Jerusalem for the celebration of the paschal feast; but his purpose having been changed by Divine Providence, he made other use of it.[50]

A queer story has been told regarding the Genoese emerald. At one time when the government was hard pressed for money, the Sacro Catino was offered to a rich Jew of Metz as pledge for a loan of 100,000 crowns. He was loath to take it, as he probably recognized its spurious character, and when his Christian clients forced him to accept it under threats of dire vengeance in case of refusal, he protested that they were taking a base advantage of the unpopularity of his faith, since they could not find a Christian who would make the loan. However, when some years later the Genoese were ready to redeem this precious relic, they were much puzzled to learn that a half-dozen different persons claimed to have it in their possession, the fact being that the Jew had fabricated a number of copies which he had succeeded in pawning for large sums, assuring the lender in each case that the redemption of the pledge was certain.

Among the celebrated emeralds noted by George Agricola[51] (1490–1555) was a large one preserved in a monastery near Lyons, France. This is also mentioned by Gesner, who states that it was shaped as a dish, or shallow cup, and was held to be the Holy Grail, like its rival at Genoa.[52] Another of Agricola's emeralds was somewhat smaller, but nevertheless measured nine inches in diameter and was in the chapel of St. Wenceslaus, at Prague; this may have been a chrysoprase, as at the present day many fine specimens of this stone can be seen in St. Wenceslaus, where the walls are inlaid with the

[50] Erasmi Stellæ, "Interpretamentum Gemmarum," 3d ed., Erfurti et Lipsiæ, 1736, p. 27.

[51] Agricolæ, "De natura fossilium," lib. vi, Basileæ, 1546, p. 289.

[52] Gesner, "De figuris lapidum," Tiguri, 1565, ff. 112v, 113r.

golden green gem-stone. Still another, larger than the last named, was set in the gold monstrance in Magdeburg, and was believed to have been the handle of Emperor Otho I's knife, since it was perforated. Possibly, however, the emerald, if genuine, was an Oriental stone, for it was customary to pierce rubies, sapphires, emeralds, etc., in the East so as to string them for necklaces or attach them as pendants to a jewel.

In the convent-church of St. Stephan, in Persian Armenia, erected about the middle of the seventeenth century, it is related by the French traveller Tavernier that there was preserved a cross said to be made out of the basin in which Christ washed the feet of the Apostles. Set in this cross was a white stone, and the priests asserted that when the cross was laid upon the body of one seriously ill, this stone would turn black if he were about to die, but would regain its white hue after his death.[53]

No jewelled sacred image has been the object of greater reverence than has been accorded to the rude little wooden carving popularly known as the "Sacro Bambino" or "Sacred Baby," in the old church of Ara Coeli in Rome. This figure was carved, in 1847, by a monk, out of a piece of olive-wood from one of the ancient trees growing on the Mount of Olives near Jerusalem. The carving was executed in the Holy Land and was sent thence to Italy, and although the ship bearing it was shipwrecked, this precious freight was miraculously preserved and is supposed to have been conveyed to its destination in some mysterious way. The reverence of the thousands of pilgrims who in the course of time have

[53] "Les six voyages de Jean Baptiste Tavernier," La Haye, 1718, vol. i, p. 48; Voyages en Perse, liv. i, chap. iv.

STATUE OF A MAORI WARRIOR, BY SIGURD NEANDROSS.

The base is a block of New Zealand jade from South Island, weighing three tons. It was donated by Mr. J. Pierpont Morgan to the American Museum of Natural History.

gazed with veneration upon this quaint and curious work of art, has found expression in the bestowal of a wealth of gems and jewels, including necklaces, brooches, rings, etc., with which the silken dress of the image is studded. A crown of gold adorned with precious stones rests upon the head of the olive-wood figure, which is jealously guarded by the priests and only shown to the faithful as a particular favor, except on the occasion of certain religious festivals.

One of the most renowned emeralds in the world surmounted the elaborately jewelled imperial crown that was placed upon the head of the venerated image of the Virgen del Sagrario in the Cathedral of Toledo. This emerald, of a rich green color, was cut as a perfect sphere and measured about 40 millimetres, or 1½ inches, in diameter. The crown itself was the work of the Toledan goldsmith, Don Diego Alejo de Montoya, who began his task in 1574 and devoted twelve years to its completion. It is described as being of almost pure gold and executed in the Renaissance style. Curiously chased in arabesque designs and enamelled in various colors, the framework of the crown served as a magnificent background for the gems constituting its adornment, which comprised rubies, emeralds, and Oriental pearls; a row of angels and cherubs sustained the arches which bore at their summit the allegorical figures of Faith, Hope, and Charity; upon that representing Faith rested the splendid emerald. This precious ornament was still preserved in the Cathedral in 1865, but was so carelessly guarded that it was stolen in 1869.[54]

If we are to believe the following anecdote, the em-

[54] José Ignacio Miró, "Estudio de las piedras preciosas," Madrid, 1870, pp. 135, 136.

erald disappeared at an earlier date: It is said that in 1809, during the French occupation of Spain, Marshal Junot visited this cathedral, and the emerald was pointed out to him as one of the chief glories of the shrine. As soon as the marshal's covetous glance rested upon the gem, he plucked it from its setting, remarking, coolly, to the astonished and horrified bystanders, "This belongs to me." Then, smiling and bowing, he left the cathedral with the emerald safely ensconced in his waistcoat pocket. Later, it was replaced by an imitation in glass.

The famous collection of jewels gathered together in the treasury of the Santa Casa, at Loreto, Italy, was plundered during the French occupation in 1797, and all trace of most of the magnificent ornaments has been lost. These represented the gifts of many crowned heads and titled personages; among the former was the unfortunate Henrietta Maria, wife of Charles I, who donated a golden heart-shaped jewel with the words "Jesus Maria" incrusted in diamonds. This jewel is described as being "as big as both a man's hands, opened onto two leaves, on one of which was the figure of the Blessed Virgin and on the other a portrait of the queen herself.[55] Of the many rich vestments for decorating the statue of the Virgin in the sanctuary, the most splendid was the gift of the Infanta Isabel of Flanders, and was valued at 40,000 crowns. In a seventeenth-century account by an English traveller it is thus described:[56]

> Its set thick with six rows of diamonds downe before, to the number of three thousand, and its all wrought over with a kinde of embroidery of little pearle set thick everywhere within the flowers with great round pearle, to the number twenty thousand pearles in all.

[55] Lassels, "The Voyage of Italy," Paris, 1670, Pt. II, p. 344.

[56] Lassels, l. c., p. 339.

The same writer tells us the niche in which the statue was placed was bordered with a row of precious stones of great number, size, and value, the colors being so varied that this bordering formed "a rich Iris of several colors." There is also said to have been a great pearl, set in gold, and engraved with the image of the Virgin and Child.[57] It seems probable that this was a jewel made of a baroque pearl, or pearls, completed by enamel-work so as to represent the sacred figures.

The pectoral cross worn in solemn processions by the prior of the monastery of San Lorenzo del Escorial was adorned with eight perfect emeralds, five diamonds, and five pearls. From it hung a splendid pear-shaped pearl, the gift of Philip II in 1595, and one of the finest of those acquired by this monarch. In 1740 the cross was valued at 50,000 crowns, Philip's great pearl not being included in this valuation.[58]

The monastery of Streoneshalh, later Whitby Abbey, was founded about 656 A.D. by Oswy, King of Northumbria, in fulfilment of a vow made before his victory over the pagan king Penda, at the battle of Winwidfield, fought in November, 654. St. Hilda was made abbess of this monastery, and Oswy's daughter Aelfleda took the veil and eventually, in 680, succeeded Hilda as abbess; she died in 713.[59] Tradition relates that at this early date crosses and rosaries were made for the inmates of the monastery from the jet found in the neighborhood. The "Whitby jet," so popular and fashionable in the eighteenth century, was largely derived from the same

[57] Scotto, "Itinerario d'Italia," Roma, 1747, p. 314.

[58] José Ignacio Miró, "Estudio de las piedras preciosas," Madrid, 1870, pp. 136, 137, 229.

[59] Cartularium abbathiæ de Whiteby, Surtees Soc. Pub., vol. lxix, pp. xvi–xx.

source, and since then has had several revivals, until replaced by black-stained chalcedony, the so-called onyx, and, later still, by steel carved with glass and glass itself.

In the sixteenth century jet was popularly called "black amber," and Cardano states that in his time beads of this material were made up into rosaries. He also says that curious figures made of jet were brought from Spain to Italy.[60]

Many are unaware of the fact that a number of ornamental objects made of nephrite and jadeite—unquestionably of European origin—are to be seen in the quiet little town of Perugia. These objects, collected principally in central and southern Italy, constitute the Belucci Collection, in that city. This collection also contains other specimens of worked jadeite, which must have been brought to Europe at the time of the Spanish conquest of Mexico and Peru. A very interesting example shows us the utilization of a pagan celt to form a Christian emblem. By the removal of a rectangular piece from each of the four corners of the jadeite celt, a perfect cross has been made, the back and front of which still offer the original polish given to the material centuries ago by the native American worker. The superstitious belief propagated in Europe by the returning Spanish sailors, very probably an invention of their own to enhance the value of their jade and jadeite, that these minerals were worn by the natives as a cure for diseases of the kidneys, whence the name *lapis nephriticus,* rendered the material exceptionally precious in the eyes of many, and quite possibly it may have been thought that, by transforming this object into the sacred form of the cross, a talisman would be produced that would not only effect the

---

[60] Cardani, "De subtilitate," lib. v, Basileæ, 1560, p. 370.

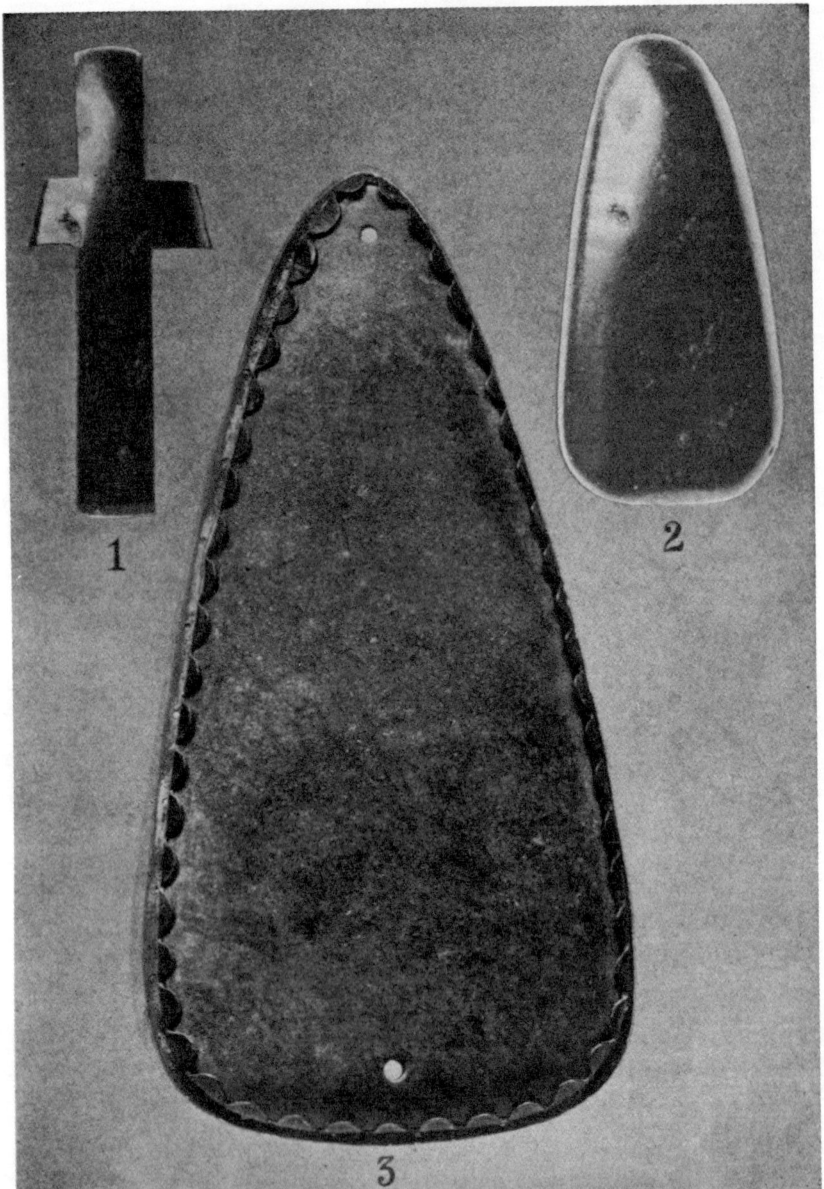

1. Cross made from a celt of jadeite (Mexican), bought from a peasant in Perugia. This was originally a celt and was divided into four pieces. Of Mexican origin and brought to Italy in sixteenth century. Belucci Collection.

2. Jadeite celt, from Guatemala.

3. Celt, Aboriginal. A small stone hatchet made of jade nephrite, of the kind believed by the peasants to be thunderbolts. Mounted in silver to be worn as a charm. This specimen, tied over the loins, is said to have been worn as recently as fifty years ago by a Scottish gentleman as a cure for kidney disease. British Museum.

cure of a special disease, but would also by its superior virtue guard the wearer from harm and danger of all kinds. Here may also be seen some celts of European jade sewed up in little bags to be worn on the loins.

Certain curious amulets called *magatama* (crooked jewels) have been found in Japanese graves of the iron age;[61] they are formed of various materials, among others of steatite, jasper, carnelian, agate, rock crystal, chrysoprase and nephrite (jade). In the shell heaps of a period preceding the iron age, the *magatama* are frequently made of horn, or of boar's or wolf's teeth, and their peculiar form, which is variously explained as a symbol, may have been conditioned by the shape of the materials originally used. The magatama were evidently regarded as amulets. "They are generally perforated at the thick end, and were worn on a string, together with beads and bugles of the same material." These peculiar ornaments were used to adorn the statues of the gods and were also employed as imperial insignia and distinctive marks of high rank. At the present day they are numbered among the three emblems of sovereignty in Japan.

A green and a red magatama are combined in the national emblem of Korea and a similar figure is used in China to symbolize the union of the masculine and feminine principles (Yang and Yin) in nature. Dr. Baelz believes that the swastika emblem, encountered in so many different parts of the world, belongs to the same order of ideas.

The Bghai tribes of Burma have many superstitions in regard to stones, such as garnets, rock-crystal, chalcedony, carnelian, agate, onyx and others of less value,

[61] Dr. Baelz, of the Imperial University of Tokyo, in Report of the Smithsonian Institution for 1904, pp. 523–547.

their repute not depending entirely or principally upon their quality as gem-stones. In almost every household is installed a stone fetish, and blood offerings are on occasion made to this. A question as to the reason for this offering elicited the following reply: "If we do not give it blood to eat it will eat us." A common belief was that spirits good or bad dwelt in the stones, and in case a great misfortune befell a family, this was sometimes laid to the charge of such a spirit. The father of a family having died, his widow commanded her son to throw away their magic stone. This he did, but the spirit was not to be denied, for shortly afterward this very stone was found to have returned to its accustomed place, and had even brought two companion stones with it![62]

Ruy Gonzalez de Clavijo, who travelled in the East during the years 1403–1406, gives a description of a slab of stone bearing the outlines of a "natural picture," and placed in the church of St. Sophia, in Constantinople:[63]

> In the wall, on the left-hand side, there is a very large white slab, on which, among many other figures, was drawn, very naturally, without any human artifice of sculpture or painting, the most sacred and blessed Virgin Mary, with our Lord Jesus Christ in her most holy arms, with his most glorious forerunner, St. John the Baptist, on one side. These images, as I said before, are not drawn or painted with any color, or inlaid, but the stone itself gave birth to this picture, with its veins, which may be clearly seen; and they say that when this stone was cut, to be placed in this most holy place, the workman saw these most wonderful and fortunate images on it, and, as this church was the most important one in the city, that stone was deposited in it. The said images appear as if they were in the clouds of heaven, and as if there was a thin veil before them.

[62] Mason, "Burmah, its People and Natural Productions," Rangoon, 1860, pp. 109, 110.

[63] Narrative of the Embassy of Ruy Gonzalez de Clavijo to the Court of Timour, trans. by Clement R. Markham, London, 1859, p. 38, Hakluyt Soc. Pub.

Many other examples of these "natural gems" are noted by early writers. Among them was an agate gem in the treasury of the Basilica of St. Mark, in Venice. Upon this gem appeared the head of a king, adorned with a diadem, the whole design being figured naturally by the veining of the agate, and not owing anything to artifice. In the same city, upon a column in the church of San Georgio Maggiore, could be seen the likeness of Our Lord, hanging from the Cross.[64]

Such stones, with peculiar markings indicating the form of human heads and figures, were regarded as the work of higher powers.

Another remarkable example is described by Kircher as follows: [65]

> In Rome, in the Chapel of the Sacred Virgin, near the organ to the right hand of those who enter the Church of St. Peter, an image may be seen in which the Blessed Virgin of Loreto is so artistically depicted by Nature that it appears to be the work of an artist's hand. She is attired in a triple garment, divided by a zone, and holds in her arms the child, who is distinguished by a crown, as is the mother. Around may be seen the figures of angels.

The red spots upon the bloodstone were said in Christian legend to represent the blood of Christ. This idea has been beautifully utilized in some gems cut from this stone, whereon the thorn-crowned head of Christ is so placed that the red spots of the bloodstone figure the drops of blood trickling down the hair and face of the Saviour. Such a gem might well be looked upon as a Christian amulet and one that could be reverently worn by any believer.

---

[64] Chiocci, "Museum Calceolarium," Veronæ, 1622, p. 251.

[65] Kircher, "Mundus Subterraneus," Amstelodami, 1665, p. 36; Tabula IV, Fig. 6.

The ignorance in the Middle Ages of the art of gem-engraving often induced the belief that engraved stones were the work of nature. A striking instance of this was the celebrated stone over the figure of the Mother of Jesus, on the tomb of St. Elizabeth of Marburg. On this gem appeared two heads touching each other, and it was, according to tradition, not a work of art, but a freak of the sculptress Nature. An oft-repeated legend tells us that a former Elector of Mainz offered the whole district of Amöneberg for this costly stone, which robber hands removed at Cassel. It is in reality a fine onyx engraved with the heads of Castor and Pollux.[66]

We might be disposed to regard rather sceptically the tales regarding wonderful stones bearing the image of Christ, or that of the Virgin Mary, and we may be inclined to believe that the old accounts are exaggerated or distorted by the pious imaginations of the writers. Nevertheless, in our own time we have a well-attested case of the discovery of such a stone.

In 1880, while visiting the village of Oberammergau, Bavaria, to witness the Passion Play, Mrs. Eugenia Jones-Bacon, of Atlanta, Georgia, found on Mount Kopfel, which overlooks the village, a small stone composed of chert and limestone, and having on its surface excrescences so disposed that, when the stone was held at a certain angle, the shadows cast by them formed a striking likeness of the head of Christ as depicted in Christian art. This peculiar freak specimen has been carefully examined by experts and has been pronounced to be entirely a work of nature. The mineralogist is not disposed to see here anything more than coincidence, and

---

[66] Creuzer, "Antik geschnittene Steine vom Grabmahl der heiligen Elizabeth," Leipsic and Darmstadt, 1834, p. 25.

yet the most sceptical cannot fail to be impressed by the fact that such a stone was found at the time and place of the Passion Play. As Max Müller said, in commenting on this strange discovery: "The chapter of accidents is much larger than we imagine," and the present writer feels disposed to add that it is remarkable how often we find what we are looking for, especially if we are only looking or thinking of one object or subject.

The religious symbolism of the diamond was a favorite theme with the thirteenth century "lapidaria," or rhymed treatises on precious stones. Just as it could only be discovered by night—an old fancy—so was the Incarnation a hidden mystery; it gave forth a great light, just as Jesus illumined the depths of Hades when he descended thither; it was unconquerably hard, and who can resist the might of God?[67]

The mediæval Italians who were fond of seeking some hidden and significant meaning in the names of precious stones, in the case of the diamond (diamante), read the phrase *amante di Dio,* or "lover of God."[68] This was a reason for regarding the brilliant gem as a sacred stone and one especially suitable for religious use.

The Rosicrucians, who sought to combine pagan with Christian types and figures, saw in the amethyst and the amethystine color a symbol of the divine male sacrifice, since the stone and the color were typical of love, truth, passion, suffering, and hope. The love of Christ led him to make the supreme sacrifice and suffer the agony of the Cross, and the Crucifixion was followed by

[67] Barbier de Montault, "Le Trésor de l'Abbaye de Sainte-Croix de Poitier"; in Mém. de la Soc. d'Antiq. de l'Ouest, Sec. Ser., vol. lv, 1881, pp. 105, 106; Poitiers, 1882.

[68] Italian MS. of the fourteenth century in the author's library; fol. 41 b.

the Resurrection, whence came the hope of mankind to enjoy eternal happiness in heaven.

The chiastolite, or macle, shows the representation of a cross on its surface, this effect being produced by the regular arrangement of carbonaceous impurities along the axes of the crystal. The name signifies a marking resembling the Greek letter *X* (chi). This marking is often very striking in appearance, and the crystal was naturally regarded as having a mystical and religious significance. It was said to stanch the flow of blood from any part of the body if worn so as to touch the skin, and it was also believed to increase the secretion of milk. All kinds of fevers were cured by this mineral if it were worn suspended from the neck, and the divine symbol it bore served to drive away evil spirits from the neighborhood of the wearer.

This very interesting mineral occurs very frequently in mica schists. When found, it appears about the thickness of a small finger, tapering slightly at each edge. If broken near one end, it often shows a white cross with a veined outline of black, making a distinct cross with black markings. The crystals frequently measure from two to four inches in length, and are found in Massachusetts, California, and other places. If small segments are broken off, it will be found that the black outline will become stronger, and the white less marked, until finally a black cross will appear, with white markings. The white material is the result of two white wedges pushed point onward until the ends meet, the narrow end of one wedge being crossed by the broad end of the second wedge, and the black filling in the balance of the square. No two of these square crosses can thus ever be exactly alike, and, when polished, the crystals naturally form an interesting stone that was known as *lapis crucifer,* or cross-stone by the ancients.

The peculiar form of the mineral known as staurolite (from the Greek σταυρός cross) is due to the twinning of two crystals at right angles. In Cronstedt's treatise on mineralogy, published in Stockholm in 1758, we are told that the staurolite was sometimes called Baseler Tauf-stein (baptismal-stone) or *lapis crucifer,* the former name being used in Basel, where the stone was employed as an amulet at baptisms. However, the *lapis crucifer* of De Boot appears from his description to have been the chias-tolite. In Brittany these twin crystals were worn as charms, and local legends state that they had dropped from the heavens.

Fine crystals of staurolite have been found in Patrick County, Virginia, and there is said to be a beautiful local legend in regard to their origin. Near where they are found there wells up a spring of limpid water, and the story goes that one day, long, long ago, when the fairies were dancing and playing around this spring, an elfin messenger winged his way through the air and alighted among them. He bore to them the sad tidings of the crucifixion of Christ in a far-off city. So mournful was his recital of the sufferings of the Saviour that the fairies burst into tears, and these fairy tear-drops, as they fell to earth, crystallized into the form of the cross. These natural crosses are in great demand as charms, and ex-President Roosevelt is said to wear one of them mounted as a watch-charm.

There has been found in the southern part of New Mexico, and in northern Mexico, a blue variety of cala-mine, a hydrous silicate of zinc, colored blue by an admix-ture of copper. This stone has been cut into gem form and has been sold to a certain extent as a cheap gem. It is translucent and is sometimes veined with white wavy lines. The Mexican Indians employed in the mines often set up a cross and a candle near where they are working, so that they may pay their devotions at this improvised shrine. In Sonora and Western Chihuahua the Indians frequently place a piece of the stone to which we have alluded alongside the cross. They may be attracted by its beautiful blue color, or they may believe that it is a turquoise, although it does not resemble this latter stone, which is more opaque, of a different shade of blue and of a different composition.

In some epitaphs the hope of the resurrection finds expression in likening the body enclosed in its narrow coffin to a precious jewel in its casket. The following lines from a tombstone erected in 1655 to the memory of Mary Courtney, at Fowell, Cornwall, England, give a good example of this class of inscription:[69]

> Near this a rare jewell's set,
> Clos'd up in a cabinet.
> Let no sacrilegious hand
> Breake through—'tis ye strickte comaund
> Of the jeweller: who hath sayd
> (And 'tis fit he be obey'd)
> I'll require it safe and sound
> Both above and under ground.

In a churchyard at Prittlewell, Essex, England, a rather whimsical treatment of the same idea is offered by some verses engraved on the stone marking the graves of two wives of a certain Freeborne, the first of whom died in 1641 and the second in 1658. The bereaved hus-

[69] Ravenshaw, "Antiente Epitaphs," London, 1878, p. 110.

STAUROLITE CRYSTALS (FAIRY STONES).
Patrick County, Virginia.

band seems to have been perfectly willing to await the Day of Judgment for the return of his lost spouses:[70]

Under this stone two precious gems do ly
Equall in weight, worth, lustre, sanctity:
Yet perhaps one of them do excell;
Which was't who knows? ask him y^{t} knew y^{em} well
By long enjoyment. If he thus be prest,
He'el pause, then answere: truly both were best:
Were't in my choice that either of ye twain
Might be returned to me to enjoy agayne,
Which should I chuse? Well, since I know not whether;
Ile mourne for the losse of both, but wish for neither,
Yet here's my comfort, herein lyes my hope,
The tyme a comeinge cabinets shall ope
Which are lockt fast: then shall I see
My Jewells to my joy, my Jewells mee.

The Christian symbolism of colors has in many cases determined the use of certain colored gems for religious ornaments, and therefore the following summary of their principal significance is of interest here:[71]

White is regarded as the first of the canonical colors, and as emblematic of purity, innocence, virginity, faith, life, and light. For this reason it is used in the ceremonies of Easter and Christmas, as in those of the Circumcision and Epiphany of Our Lord. As the color of virginity it is especially appropriate for the festival of the Virgin Mary, and as that of faith not sealed with blood, for the festivals of the saints who were not martyred. The heavenly host of angels and saints wear white robes, and in pictures of the Assumption of the Virgin she is frequently clad in white.

Red is used at the feasts of the Exaltation and Invention of the Cross, at Pentecost, and at the Feast of Martyrs. It suggests and symbolizes suffering and martyrdom for the faith, and the supreme

[70] Ravenshaw, "Antiente Epitaphs," London, 1878, p. 113.

[71] See Audsley, "Handbook of Christian Symbolism," London, 1865, pp. 135–137.

sacrifice of Christ upon the Cross. Divine love and majesty are also typified by this color.

Blue is an emblem of the celestial regions and of the celestial virtues. Nevertheless, as this is not one of the five canonical colors, it is not employed for the decoration of churches or for ecclesiastical vestments. In Christian art, however, the Virgin and the saints and angels are often robed in blue.

Yellow of a golden hue is emblematic of God's goodness and of faith and good works, but it is not a canonical color. A dull yellow, however, has the opposite signification, and is a type of treachery and envy. Hence Judas is garbed in yellow of a dull hue, and heretics wore garments of this shade when they were condemned to the stake.

Green is the canonical color for use on Sundays, week-days, and ordinary festivals. Hope and joy and the bright promises of youth are signified by green.

Violet, another canonical color, is appropriate for use on Septuagesima and Quinquagesima Sundays, during Lent, and on Advent Sunday. The chastening and purifying effects of suffering find expression in this color.

Black, also a canonical color, is a symbol of death and of the mourning and sorrow inspired by death. Therefore it is only used in the Church on Good Friday, to symbolize the sorrow and despair of the Christian community at the death of Christ, a sorrow soon to be turned to joy by His glorious resurrection.

FRONTISPIECE OF THE "VESTITUS SACERDOTUM HEBRÆORUM," OF JOHANN BRAUN, AMSTERDAM, 1680.

The vignettes at the top illustrate the source of the materials of the vestments, etc.; as the nopal, source of the cochineal insect; gold-thread; linen; a sheep for wool; Tyre and the purple murex. The other vignettes show separate parts of the high-priest's attire, and in the centre appear two figures of the high-priest, each garbed in different sets of vestments.

II

On the High-Priest's Breastplate

VERY early, and very naturally, the religious nature of man led to the use of precious stones in connection with worship—the most valuable and elegant objects being chosen for sacred purposes. Of this mode of thought, we have a striking instance in the accounts given, in the book of Exodus, of the breastplate of the High-priest, and the gems contributed for the tabernacle by the Israelites in the wilderness. Another religious association of such objects is their use to symbolize ideas of the Divine glory, as illustrated in the visions of the prophet Ezekiel and in the description of the New Jerusalem in the book of Revelation. Apart from such legitimate uses, however, gems have become associated with all manner of religious fancies and superstitions, traces of which appear in the Talmud, the Koran, and similar writings; they have also been dedicated to various heathen deities. Even in modern times, some trace of the same ideas remains in the ecclesiastical jewelry and its supposed symbolism.

In the vision of Ezekiel i, 26, and in a brief allusion to the similar appearance of the God of Israel in Exodus xxiv, the throne of Jehovah, or the pavement beneath his feet, is compared to a sapphire, and the Apostle John, in the Apocalypse, describes the Great White Throne as surrounded by a rainbow like an emerald.

The Rabbinical writings, instead of the simple grandeur of these biblical comparisons, give us many fanciful ideas. The stones of the breastplate are here represented as sacred to twelve mighty angels who guard the gates of

Paradise, and wondrous tales are told of the luminous gems in the tent of Abraham and the ark of Noah. Mohammedan legend represents the different heavens as composed of different precious stones, and in the Middle Ages these religious ideas became interwoven with a host of astrological, alchemistic, and medical superstitions.

The following is the description of the breastplate given in Exodus (xxviii, 15–30):

> And thou shalt make the breastplate of judgment with cunning work; after the work of the ephod thou shalt make it; of gold, of blue, and of purple, and of scarlet, and of fine twined linen shalt thou make it.
>
> Foursquare it shall be being doubled; a span shall be the length thereof, and a span shall be the breadth thereof.
>
> And thou shalt set in it settings of stones, even four rows of stones: the first row shall be a sardius, a topaz, and a carbuncle: this shall be the first row.
>
> And the second row shall be an emerald, a sapphire, and a diamond.
>
> And the third row a ligure, an agate, and an amethyst.
>
> And the fourth row a beryl, and an onyx, and a jasper; they shall be set in gold in their enclosings.
>
> And the stones shall be with the names of the children of Israel, twelve, according to their names, like the engravings of a signet; every one with his name shall they be according to the twelve tribes.
>
> And thou shalt make upon the breastplate chains at the ends of wreathen work of pure gold.
>
> And thou shalt make upon the breastplate two rings of gold, and shalt put the two rings on the two ends of the breastplate.
>
> And thou shalt put the two wreathen chains of gold in the two rings which are on the ends of the breastplate.
>
> And the other two ends of the two wreathen chains thou shalt fasten in the two ouches, and put them on the shoulder-pieces of the ephod before it.
>
> And thou shalt make two rings of gold, and thou shalt put them upon the two ends of the breastplate in the border thereof, which is in the side of the ephod inward.

And two other rings of gold thou shalt make, and shalt put them on the two sides of the ephod underneath, toward the forepart thereof, over against the other coupling thereof, above the curious girdle of the ephod.

And they shall bind the breastplate by the rings thereof unto the rings of the ephod with a lace of blue, that it may be above the curious girdle of the ephod, and that the breastplate be not loosed from the ephod.

And Aaron shall bear the names of the children of Israel in the breastplate of judgment upon his heart, when he goeth in unto the holy place, for a memorial before the Lord continually.

And thou shalt put in the breastplate of Judgment the Urim and the Thummim; and they shall be upon Aaron's heart, when he goeth in before the Lord: and Aaron shall bear the judgment of the children of Israel upon his heart before the Lord continually.

Of the miraculous quality of the stones worn by the high-priest, the Jewish historian Josephus (37–95 A.D.) says:[1]

From the stones which the high-priest wore (these were sardonyxes, and I hold it superfluous to describe their nature, since it is known to all), there emanated a light, as often as God was present at the sacrifices; that which was worn on the right shoulder instead of a clasp emitting a radiance sufficient to give light even to those far away, although the stone previously lacked this splendor. And certainly this in itself merits the wonder of all those who do not, out of contempt for religion, allow themselves to be led away by a pretence of wisdom. However, I am about to relate something still more wonderful, namely, that God announced victory in battle by means of the twelve stones worn by the high-priest on his breast, set in the pectoral. For such a splendor shone from them when the army was not yet in motion, that all the people knew that God himself was present to aid them. For this reason the Greeks who reverence our solemnities, since they could not deny this, called the pectoral λόγιον or oracle. However, the pectoral and the onyxes ceased to emit this radiance two hundred years before the time when I write this, because God was displeased at the transgressions of the Law.

---

[1] Flavii Josephi, "De Antiq. Jud.," lib. iii, cap. viii, 9; Opera, ed. Dindorf, Parisiis, 1845, vol. i, pp. 100, 101.

This writer, who must have seen the high-priest wearing his elaborate vestments, says that the breastplate was adorned "with twelve stones of exceptional size and beauty, a decoration not easily to be acquired, on account of its enormous value."[2] However these gems were not merely rare and costly; they also possessed wonderful and miraculous powers. Writing about 400 A.D., St. Epiphanius, Bishop of Constantia, tells of a marvellous *adamas* which was worn on the breast of the high-priest, who showed himself to the people, arrayed in all his gorgeous vestments, at the feasts of Pascha, Pentecost, and Tabernacles. This adamas was termed the δήλωσις or "Declaration," because, by its appearance, it announced to the people the fate that God had in store for them. If the people were sinful and disobedient, the stone assumed a dusky hue, which portended death by disease, or else it became the color of blood, signifying that the people would be slain by the sword. If, however, the stone shone like the driven snow, then the people recognized that they had not sinned, and hastened to celebrate the festival.[3]

There seems to be little doubt that this account is nothing more than an elaboration and modification of the passage in Josephus. Evidently the λόγιον (oracle) of Josephus has become the δήλωσις (declaration).

When Moses wished to engrave on the stones of the breastplate the names of the twelve tribes of Israel, he is said to have had recourse to the miraculous *shamir*. The names were first traced in ink on the stones, and the *shamir* was then passed over them, the result being that

---

[2] "Ant. Jud.," lib. iii, cap. vii, 5, Flavii Josephi Opera, Basileæ, 1544, p. 75.

[3] Sancti Patri Epiphanii, "De XII Gemmis," Tiguri, 1566, ff. 12–14. Edited by Conrad Gesner from a unique MS. in his possession.

THE HEBREW HIGH-PRIEST ATTIRED WITH HIS VESTMENTS.
(From Johann Braun's "Vestitus Sacerdotum Hebraeorum," Amsterdam, 1680, opp. p. 822.)

the traced inscriptions became graven on the stones. In proof of the magical character of this operation, no particles of the gems were removed in the process.[4] The name really designates "emery."

An argument against the use of especially rare and costly stones in the decoration of the breastplate has been found in its probable size.[5] We are told that when folded it measured a span in each direction, and this would indicate that its length and breadth were each from eight to nine inches. In this case the stones themselves might have measured two by two and a half inches, and, in view of the number of characters required to express some of the tribal names, these dimensions do not seem excessive. It is highly improbable that in the time of Moses precious stones like the ruby, the emerald, or the sapphire would have been available in these dimensions. The difficulty of engraving very hard stones with the appliances at the command of the Hebrews of this period must also be taken into consideration. As we shall see, however, there is good reason to believe that after the Babylonian Captivity a new breastplate was made, and at that time it may have been easier to secure and work precious stones of great value and a high degree of hardness. We must also bear in mind that in those periods perfection was not so great a requisite as rich color.

In his commentary on Exodus xxviii, Cornelius à Lapide (Cornelius Van den Steen) discusses the question of the diamond in the high-priest's breastplate. In the first place, he notes that the diamond was very costly, and

---

[4] Ginsburg, "Legends of the Jews," Eng. trans., Phila., 1909, vol. i, p. 34.

[5] See J. L. Myers in the "Encyclopædia Biblica," vol. iv, pp. 4799–4812.

that a large stone would have been needed to bear the name of Judah or that of any other tribe. He considers that a stone of the requisite size would have cost a hundred thousand gold crowns, and he asks, "Whence could

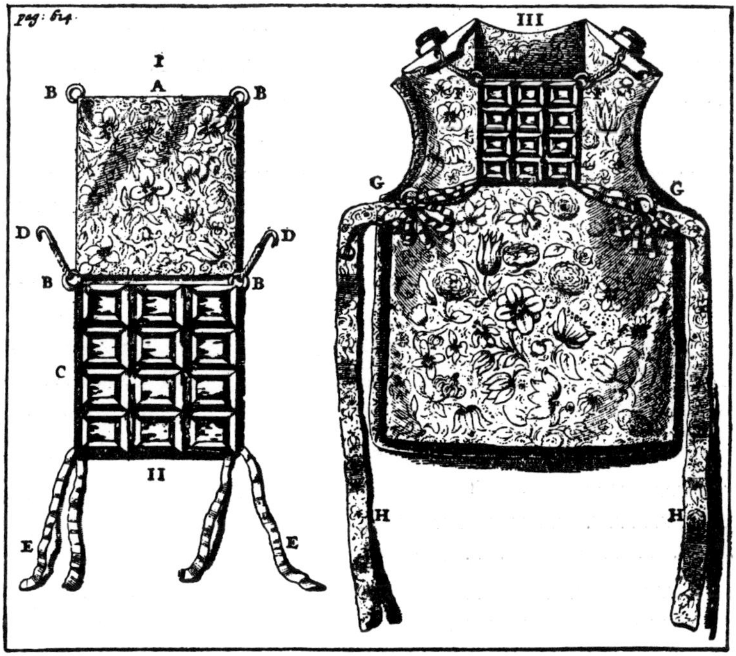

I, II, THE BREASTPLATE UNFOLDED.

A, lower fold; *B*, *B*, *B*, *B*, rings for attachment to Ephod; *C*, the twelve gems in their settings; *D*, *D*, hooks for attachment to shoulder; *E*, *E*, bands to pass through rings in Ephod.

III. EPHOD WITH BREASTPLATE FOLDED AND ATTACHED.

G, *G*, rings through which pass bands of Breastplate; *H*, *H*, bands of Ephod. From Johann Braun's "Vestitus Sacerdotum Hebraeorum," Amsterdam, 1680.

the poor Hebrews have obtained such a sum of money, and where could they have found such a diamond?" He proceeds to give still another reason for doubting that the diamond was in the breastplate,—namely, that it would have marked too great a distinction between the tribes, the result being that the tribe to which the diamond was assigned would have been puffed up with pride, while the others would have been filled with hatred and envy, "for the diamond is the Queen Gem of all the gems."[6]

The use of the breastplate to reveal the guilt of an offender is testified to in a Samaritan version of the book of Joshua, which has been discovered by Dr. Moses Gaster, chief rabbi of the Spanish and Portuguese Jews in England. According to this version, Achan steals a golden image from a heathen temple in Jericho. The high-priest's breastplate reveals his guilt, for the stones lose their light and grow dim when his name is pronounced.

Many conjectures have been made as to the origin of the breastplate with the mystic Urim and Thummim enclosed within it. That an Egyptian origin should be sought seems most probable. A breast-ornament worn by the high-priest of Memphis, as figured in an Egyptian relief, consists of twelve small balls, or crosses, intended to represent Egyptian hieroglyphics. As it cannot be determined that these figures were cut from precious stones, the only definite connection with the Hebrew ornament is the number of the figures; this suggests, but fails to prove, a common origin. The monuments show that the high-priest of Memphis wore this ornament as early as the fourth Dynasty, or, approximately, 4000 B.C.[7]

Of the Urim and Thummim, the mysterious oracle of the ancient Hebrews, St. Augustine (354–450 A.D.), after acknowledging the great difficulty of interpreting the

---

[6] See Gimma, "Della storia naturale delle gemme," Napoli, 1730, vol. i, pp. 208, 209.

[7] Hommel, "Altisraelitische Ueberlieferung," pp. 281, sqq.; Erman, "Aegypten," Tübingen, 1885, p. 402.

meaning of the words and the character of the oracle, adds that some believed the words to signify a single stone which changed color according as the answer was favorable or unfavorable, while the priest was entering the sanctuary; still he thought it possible that merely the letters of the words Urim and Thummin were inscribed upon the breastplate.[8]

After the capture of Jerusalem by Titus in 70 A.D., the treasures of the temple were carried off to Rome, and we learn from Josephus that the breastplate was deposited in the Temple of Concord, which had been erected by Vespasian. Here it is believed to have been at the time of the sacking of Rome by the Vandals under Genseric, in 455, although Rev. C. W. King thinks it is not improbable that Alaric, king of the Visigoths, when he sacked Rome in 410 A.D., might have secured this treasure.[9] However, the express statement of Procopius that "the vessels of the Jews" were carried through the streets of Constantinople, on the occasion of the Vandalic triumph of Belisarius, in 534, may be taken as a confirmation of the conjecture that the Vandals had secured possession of the breastplate and its jewels.[10]

It must, however, be carefully noted that Procopius nowhere mentions the breastplate and that it need not have been included among "the vessels of the Jews." It appears that this part of the spoils of Belisarius was placed by Justinian (483–565) in the sacristy of the church of St. Sophia. Some time later, the emperor is said to have heard of the saying of a certain Jew to the

---

[8] Aureli Augustini, "Opera Omnia," vol. iii, Part I, col. 637; Patrologiæ Latinæ, ed. Migne, vol. xxxviii, Paris, 1864.

[9] "Natural History of Precious Stones," London, 1870, p. 333.

[10] Procopius, ed. Dindorf, Bonnae. 1833, vol. i, p. 445; "De bello Vandalico," lib. ii, cap. 9.

effect that, until the treasures of the Temple were restored to Jerusalem, they would bring misfortune upon any place where they might be kept.[11] If this story be true, Justinian may have felt that the fate of Rome was a lesson for him, and that Constantinople must be saved from a like disaster. Moved by such considerations, he is said to have sent the "sacred vessels" to Jerusalem, and they were placed in the Church of the Holy Sepulchre.

This brings us to the last two events which can be even plausibly connected with the mystic twelve gems,—namely, the capture and sack of Jerusalem by the Sassanian Persian king, Khusrau II, in 615, and the overthrow of the Sassanian Empire by the Mohammedan Arabs, and the capture and sack of Ctesiphon, in 637.[12] If we admit that Khusrau took the sacred relics of the Temple with him to Persia, we may be reasonably sure that they were included among the spoils secured by the Arab conquerors, although King, who has ingeniously endeavored to trace out the history of the breastplate jewels after the fall of Jerusalem in 70 A.D., believes that they may be still "buried in some unknown treasure-chamber of one of the old Persian capitals."

A fact which has generally been overlooked by those who have embarked on the sea of conjecture relative to the fate of the breastplate stones is that a large Jewish contingent, numbering some twenty-six thousand men, formed part of the force with which the Sassanian Persians captured Jerusalem, and they might well lay claim

[11] Procopius, ed. Dindorf, Bonnae, 1833, vol. i, p. 445; "De bello Vandalico," lib. ii, cap. 9.

[12] For an account of the immense booty taken by the Arabs, under Sa'ad, on this occasion, see Rawlinson, "Seventh Great Oriental Monarchy," London, 1876, pp. 564–566. The total value has been placed as high as $125,000,000.

to any Jewish vessels or jewels that may have been secured by the conquerors. In this case, however, it is still probable that these precious objects fell into the hands of the Mohammedans who captured Jerusalem in the same year in which they took Ctesiphon.

One circumstance which may have contributed to the preservation of these gems in their original form after they fell into the hands of the Romans is the fact that each one was engraved with the name of one of the Jewish tribes, the inscription being probably in the older form of Hebrew writing, which was used in the coinage even as late as the last revolt in 137 A.D. Hence, recutting would have been necessary to fit them for use as ornaments, a process not easily accomplished, and involving a great loss of size. We must also bear in mind that the intrinsic value of the gems may not have been so great as many suppose, since all of them were probably of the less perfect forms of the precious and semi-precious varieties. It is very likely that the enthusiastic statements of Josephus in this connection were dictated by national pride, or arose from the tendency to exaggeration so common among the Oriental writers. Certainly, if the breastplate known to Josephus was made not long after the return of the Jews from the Babylonian Captivity, their financial resources at the time of its fabrication were quite restricted.

Admitting as a possibility that the Arabs may have secured possession of the breastplate, how would they have regarded it? The heroes of the Old Testament, and especially Moses, were such sacred personalities in the eyes of Mohammedans that this relic would have been as precious for them as for us. However, the victorious Arabs who overran the Sassanian Empire, although filled with religious zeal, were no students of archæology, and would have been quite unable to decipher the strange characters engraved on the stones. They would most probably have supposed them to be Persian characters, and would, therefore, have valued these stones no higher than others in the Persian treasure. This can serve as an explanation of the fact that no allusion to the breastplate with its adornment can be found in the works of those Mohammedan writers, such as Tabari, who treat of the overthrow of the Sassanian Empire. We may be sure that the Persians themselves would have accorded no special honor to objects connected with the Hebrew religion, since their own Zoroastrian faith had no connection with it.

In 628, not long before the date of the Arab invasion, the most precious relic of Christendom, the cross discovered by Helena, mother of Constantine the Great, and believed to be the very cross on which Christ died, was surrendered to the Greek Emperor Heraclius by Kobad II, son of Khusrau II, on the conclusion of a treaty of peace between the Eastern and Sassanian Empires. This cross was one of the sacred objects borne away to Persia from Jerusalem by Khusrau in 615 A.D. It is said to have been guarded carefully through the influence of Sira, Khusrau's Christian wife. There is a bare possibility that other objects of religious veneration, taken from Jerusalem, may have been given up by the Persians at the same time, and that the unique character of the most important relic so overshadowed all others that historians have failed to note the fact. The cross was restored to Jerusalem by Heraclius in 629, only to fall into the hands of the Mohammedans when that city was taken by the Arabs under Omar, in 637. Hence, if the jewelled breastplate had also been surrendered by Kobad, it would probably have shared the same fate.

SILVER CROSS WITH QUARTZ CAT'S EYE.
Russian, sixteenth century. Collection of Mrs. Henry Draper.

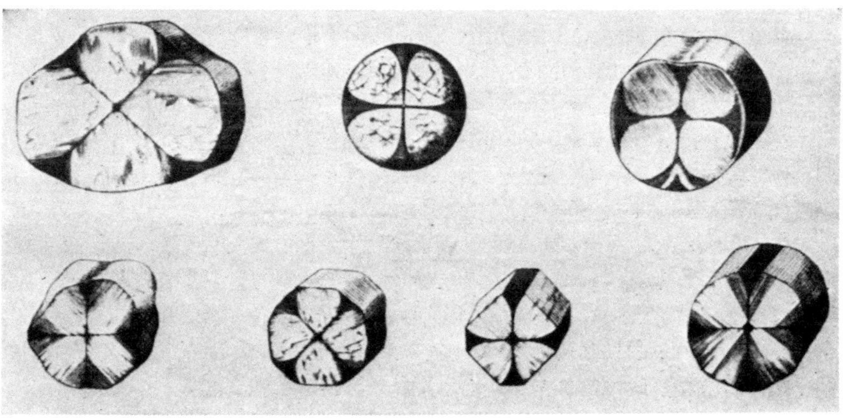

SPECIMENS OF CHIASTOLITE (LAPIS CRUCIFER). (See page 271.)
From the "Metallotheca Vaticana" of Mercatus, Rome, 1719, p. 238. In the author's library.

We have here a wide field for conjecture,—but, unfortunately, nothing more. Still, in the absence of any definite and trustworthy information, there is a kind of romantic interest in viewing the various possible relations of the mystery surrounding the fate of the most precious gems, historically at least, that have ever existed. More especially is this interest justified in the case of all who are disposed to prize gems and jewels for their symbolic significance, for, as we have shown, this significance, as far as concerns natal stones and the spiritual interpretation of the qualities of the heart and soul symbolized by the color and character of the principal precious and semi-precious stones, has its root in the veneration felt by early Christian writers, beginning with the author of the Apocalypse, for the unforgotten and unforgettable gems that were worn by the Hebrew high-priest.

A rather ingenious utilization of the reputed powers of Aaron's breastplate comes to us in a book printed in Portland, Maine.[13] The writer assumes that the Urim and Thummim enclosed in the folds of the breastplate consisted of twelve stones, duplicates of those engraved with the names of the tribes, and so disposed that, when they were shaken to and fro and then allowed to come to rest, three of them would become visible through an aperture in the ephod just beneath the rows of set stones. The signification of the oracle is given by the various combinations of color offered by the three stones that reveal themselves; to each combination a prearranged meaning is given. That anything of the kind could have been true of the original Urim and Thummim is scarcely worthy the trouble of refutation, but the

[13] C. H. Emerson, "Psychocraft" [Portland, Me., 1911].

practical result of this modern experiment is a clever oracle which will probably enjoy a certain vogue.

For those who, with the late lamented Lieutenant Totten, see in the tribes of Manasseh and Ephraim the Anglo-Saxons of England and the United States, and who look upon George V as the king who sits upon the throne of David, these symbolical stones of the breastplate acquire an added significance. While not pretending to be able to follow all the intricate and certainly most ingenious and interesting speculations of this school of Biblical exegesis, we cannot help expressing some astonishment that Ephraim should be thought to prefigure England and Manasseh the United States, instead of *vice versa*. In Gen. xlviii, 17–20, the text more especially referred to in these speculations, Jacob's blessing is bestowed upon Ephraim, in spite of Joseph's protest that it should go to the *eldest* son, Manasseh. To this protest Jacob answers: "I know it, my son, I know it: he also [Manasseh] shall become a people, and he also shall be great: but truly his younger brother shall be greater than he, and his seed shall become a multitude of nations." Certainly the very composite population of the United States perfectly merits this description. As a general rule, the Hebrews, when using the names Ephraim and Manasseh as tribal designations, maintained the twelve-fold division of the people, by substituting these tribes for Joseph and by dropping the name of Levi from the list, the tribe of Levi being assigned as priests to the care of the sanctuary, and not participating in the division of the Land of Promise.

In the Midrash Bemidbar, the Rabbinical commentary on Numbers, the tribes are given in their order, with the stone appropriate to each and the color of the tribal standard pitched in the desert camp, this color corresponding in each case with that of the tribal stone. This list represents a tradition dating back to at least the twelfth century and possibly much earlier than that; hence its value should not be underestimated, although we may not accept it without some reserves.[14]

Odem	Reuben	Red
Pitdah	Simeon	Green
Bareketh	Levi	White, black and red
Jophek	Judah	Sky-blue
Sappir	Issachar	Black (like stibium)
Yahalom	Zebulun	White
Leshem	Dan	Sapphire-color
Shebo	Gad	Gray
Ahlamah	Naphtali	Wine-color
Tarshish	Assher	Pearl-color (?)
Shoham	Joseph	Very black
Yashpheh	Benjamin	Colors of all the stones

In the attempt to determine the identity of the stones enumerated in Exodus xxviii and xxxix, as adorning the breastplate of the high-priest, we must bear in mind that this "breastplate of Aaron" and the one described by Josephus, and brought by Titus to Rome after the capture of Jerusalem in 70 A.D., are in all probability entirely distinct objects. The former, if it ever existed, except in the ideal world of the authors of the Priestly Codex, must have been composed of the stones known to and used by the Egyptians of the thirteenth or fourteenth century, B.C., some of them being, perhaps, set in the "jewels of gold and jewels of silver" borrowed by the Israelites from the Egyptians just before the Exodus; on the other hand, the most trustworthy indications re-

[14] "Der Midrasch Bemidbar Rabba," German transl. by Dr. Aug. Wünsche, Leipzig, 1885, pp. 15, 16. Parasha II. Of the *tarshish* it is said the color resembled that of "the costly stone with which women adorn themselves," possibly the pearl is signified. Hebrew text in "Sepher Midrash Rabba," Vilna, 1845, pt. iii, "Sepher Bemidbar," p. 23.

garding the stones of the breastplate of the Second Temple, made perhaps in the fifth century B.C., should be sought in the early Greek and Latin versions of the Old Testament, and in the treatise on precious stones by Theophrastus, who wrote about 300 B.C. The Natural History of Pliny, that great storehouse of ancient knowledge, and other early writers, may also be used with profit.

TITLE PAGE OF THE EDITION OF MARBODUS ON PRECIOUS STONES, PUBLISHED IN COLOGNE, 1539.

Shows the figure of the High-priest and the names and tribal attributions of twelve stones of the Breastplate.

I. Odem. [אֹדֶם.] The etymology of this word clearly indicates that we have to do with a red stone, most probably the carnelian. We know that in ancient Egypt hieroglyphic texts from the Book of the Dead were engraved upon amulets made from this stone, and it was also used for early Babylonian cylinders. Fine specimens of carnelian were obtained from Arabia. The Greek Septuagint and the Latin Vulgate, as well as Josephus, in the "Wars of the Jews" (V, 5, 7), and Epiphanius, all translate *sardius,* the ancient designation of carnelian; in his "Antiquities," however, Josephus renders *odem* by "sardonyx." The Egyptian word *chenem* was used to designate red stones, and seems to have been applied indifferently to red jasper and red feldspar as well as to carnelian; indeed, the first-named material was more freely used in early Egyptian work than the carnelian. It is, therefore, probable that in Mosaic times *odem* signified red jasper, while for the fifth century B.C. "carnelian" would be the better rendering. This modern name of the *sardius,* signifying the "flesh-colored" stone, first appears in the Latin translation of a treatise by Luca ben Costa, who wrote in the tenth century A.D. The name of Reuben is said to have been engraved on the *odem* stone, which occupied the first place on the breastplate.

II. Pitdah. [פִּטְדָה.] There seems to be little doubt that this is the *topazius* of ancient writers, which usually signified our chrysolite, or peridot, not our topaz; for Pliny and his successors describe the topazius as a stone of a greenish hue. A legend related by Pliny gives as the place of origin an island in the Red Sea, called Topazos, from *topazein,* "to conjecture," because it was difficult to find. However, the Hebrew *pitdah* appears to have been derived from the Sanskrit *pita,* "yellow," and should, therefore, have originally signified a yellow stone, perhaps our topaz. W. M. Flinders Petrie, probably influenced by this Sanskrit etymology, sees in it the yellow serpentine used in ancient Egypt. If, nevertheless, we admit that a light green stone occupied the second place on the Mosaic breastplate, it was perhaps the light green serpentine. This was called *meh* in Egyptian, and was often used for amulets. In the case of the later breastplate we may substitute the peridot. On this second stone was engraved the name Simeon.

III. Bareketh. [בָּרֶקֶת.] Here the Septuagint, Josephus, and the Vulgate agree in translating *smaragdus,* and as we know that emerald mines were worked at

Mount Zabarah, in Nubia, before the beginning of our era, and that the emerald was known and used in Egypt, there does not seem to be any reason for rejecting the usual translation "emerald." Still it must be admitted that *smaragdus* often designates other green stones than the emerald. The suggestion has been made (by Myers and Petrie) that the passage in Revelation iv, 3, where the rainbow is likened to the *smaragdus,* indicates that the writer used this name for rock-crystal; but this conjecture is scarcely satisfactory, since it confuses the prismatic effects of light which has traversed the crystal with the crystal itself. There can be little doubt that a stone of brilliant coloration, like the emerald, not a colorless one, like rock-crystal, would be used as a simile of the rainbow. Whether the Mosaic breastplate already contained the emerald is another question, and it seems rather more likely that green feldspar, freely used in ancient Egypt for amulets, and known as *uat,* was the third stone of the proto-breastplate. The Authorized Version makes "the carbuncle" the third instead of the fourth stone. Upon the *bereketh* was engraved the name Levi.

IV. Nophek. [נֹפֶךְ.] This name is rendered ἄνθραξ by the Septuagint and Josephus, and "carbunculus" by the Vulgate. This designation, signifying literally "a glowing coal," was used for certain stones distinguished by their peculiarly brilliant red color, such as the ruby and certain fine garnets. While it is quite possible that the Oriental ruby may have been in the breastplate seen by Josephus, it is almost certain that it could not have been in the original breastplate of Mosaic times, since there is absolutely no proof that this stone was known in ancient Egypt. Hence we are inclined to believe that in the thirteenth century B.C. the name *nophek* designated

CROSS, ATTACHED AS PENDANT TO THE CROWN OF THE GOTHIC KING RECCESVINTHUS (649-672 A.D.).

Forming part of the treasure discovered in 1858 at Guarrazar in Spain. Now in Musée Cluny, Paris. The cross proper is set with fine sapphires cut en cabochon and eight large pearls. Natural size.

the almandine garnet, or some similar variety of that stone. The Authorized Version has "emerald" here instead of in the third place. On this fourth stone of the breastplate was engraved the tribal name of Judah.

V. Sappir. [סַפִּיר.] This is rendered *sapphirus* in all the old versions.[15] The stone cannot have been our sapphire, for both Theophrastus and Pliny describe the *sapphirus* as a stone with golden spots, thus showing that they meant the lapis-lazuli, which is often spotted with particles of pyrites having a golden sheen. This stone was named *chesbet* by the Egyptians, and was highly prized by them, a quantity of lapis-lazuli often appearing as an important item in the lists of tribute paid to Egypt and among the gifts sent by Babylonia to the Egyptian monarchs, and obtained from the oldest mines in the world. These were worked at a period 4000 B.C. and still are worked to this day. From this material amulets and figures were made, many of which have been preserved for us, and the Egyptian high-priest is said to have worn, suspended from his neck, an image of Mat, the Goddess of Truth, made of lapis-lazuli. The name is composed of the Latin *lapis,* "a stone," and *lajuward,* the name of the stone in Persian. From this latter word is also derived our "azure." In ancient times the lapis-lazuli was the blue stone *par excellence,* because of its beautiful color and the valuable ultramarine dye derived from it. Although Pliny writes (xxxvii, 39) that this stone was too soft for engraving, this fact need not have prevented its use in the breastplate, since the stones set therein were not intended for use as seals and hence were not subjected to any wear. In this connec-

[15] There are two evident transpositions in the text of Josephus between the fifth and sixth and the eighth and ninth stones respectively.

tion, however, it is somewhat strange that the Hebrew word *sappir* appears to indicate a stone especially adapted to receive inscriptions. The fact that the lapis-lazuli was greatly esteemed in ancient Egypt, and was still much used as an ornamental stone in Greek and Roman times, renders it probable that it was set not only in the original breastplate, but also in that of a later age. Upon this fifth stone the name Issachar was inscribed.

VI. Yahalom. [יַהֲלֹם.] The sixth stone of the Septuagint version and of Josephus is the ἴασπις, probably green jasper, or jade, and this has been assumed to show that in the original Hebrew text *yashpheh* was the sixth stone, in place of *yahalom.* The twelfth stone of the Greek version is the ὀνύχιον or "onyx," and this seems to be the most probable equivalent of the Hebrew *yahalom.* Some Hebrew sources, however, render it "diamond," and Luther in his German version of the Bible, as well as our own Authorized Version, translates it thus. This rendering is based upon the derivation of the word *yahalom* from a verb meaning "to smite," thus making the name of the stone signify "the smiter," a designation not inappropriate for the diamond, which, because of its extreme hardness, has the power to cut, or "smite," all other stones. However, for this purpose the emery corundum, or smiris-point *shamir,* mentioned in Zechariah, was most likely used. The diamond was certainly not used in this way in very early times, although it is possible that the stone was employed in engraving in the fifth century B.C. These considerations induce us to prefer the traditional interpretation of *yahalom,* and translate it "onyx." In this case "the smiter" could be explained as denoting the use of the engraved onyx for sealing, as the engraved figure or letters were struck upon some soft material to make an impression. Zebulun was the tribal name inscribed on the *yahalom.*

VII. Leshem. [לֶשֶׁם.] No stone in the breastplate is more difficult to determine than this one. The Septuagint, Josephus, and the Vulgate all translate *ligurius,* an appellation sometimes applied to amber, a substance quite unfitted for use in the breastplate among the other engraved stones. Probably the original significance of *ligurius* was amber, this name being used because Liguria, in northern Italy, was the chief source of supply for Greece and the Orient; amber which had been gathered on the shores of the Baltic being brought by traders to Liguria and forwarded thence to other lands. As, however, the Greeks had another name for amber, *electron,* the name *ligurion* appears to have been applied later to a variety of the jacinth somewhat resembling amber in color, and then to other varieties of the same stone. The original form of the name was evidently *ligurion,* which was later changed to *lyncurion,* and was then explained as meaning the urine of the lynx (from λύγξ, and οὖρον, urine). This fanciful etymology gave rise to the story that the *ligurios,* or rather *lyncurius,* was the solidified urine of the lynx. The term *lyncurion,* as used by Theophrastus, may possibly have included the sapphire as well as the jacinth, since he lays especial stress upon the coldness of this substance, a quality characteristic of the sapphire, and also of the still denser jacinth. Hence, it appears that we have, even in the name *ligurius,* some justification for accepting the rendering *hyacinthus,* suggested by the list of foundation stones in Revelation xxi, 20, and already proposed by Epiphanius, Bishop of Constantia, about 400 A.D. Whether *hyacinthus* should be rendered "sapphire'' or ''jacinth'' is not easy to determine, as this name seems to have been used indifferently for both stones; with the Arabs, under the form *yakut,* it became a generic term for all the varieties of the corundum gems. The sapphire was engraved in Greek and Roman times and is, perhaps, the *leshem* stone of the Second Temple. For the Mosaic breastplate we are forced to seek for some stone known in ancient Egypt, where the sapphire does not seem to have been introduced at an early date. If we could accept the suggestion of Brugsch that the Egyptian *neshem* stone, reputed to have wonderful magic virtues, was the same as the Hebrew *leshem,* a brown agate would have been the seventh stone in the original breastplate, as Wendel gives very strong reasons for rendering *neshem* in this way. The color designations were very freely used in Egyptian, and therefore a reddish or a yellowish brown agate may have been used. The *leshem* bore the tribal name Joseph.

VIII. Shebo. [שְׁבוֹ.] This is uniformly rendered in the ancient versions and in Josephus by ''agate,'' a composite stone highly esteemed in very ancient times, and hence worthy of a place among the stones of the breastplate; at a later period, as Pliny notes (xxxvii, 54), it became so common that it was but little regarded. Nevertheless the fact that the various kinds of agates were believed to have many talismanic and therapeutic virtues, the great variety of coloration observable in these stones, and the curious figures and markings displayed by many of them, served to make them favorite objects. The etymology of the word *shebo* suggests that it designated more especially a banded agate, and that set in the proto-breastplate was most probably one with gray and white bands, as this variety often appears in Egyptian work. There would have been no lack of contrast between this stone and the reddish or yellowish-brown agate, of uniform color, which may have occupied the seventh place. For the later breastplate we may choose any one of the many kinds of banded agate. This stone had engraved upon it the name Benjamin.

IX. Aḥlamah. [אַחְלָמָה.] As to this stone also, all the authorities are in agreement, and render *aḥlamah* by "amethyst." This was not, however, the Oriental amethyst, a variety of corundum, but a dark blue or purple variety of quartz. Both Arabia and Syria furnished a supply of amethysts. The Hebrew name shows that this stone was believed to possess the virtue of inducing dreams and visions (cf. *halom*—"dream"), while, as is well known, the Greek name characterizes it as an enemy or preventive of inebriety. The amethyst was known in ancient Egypt and probably was named *hemag*. In the Book of the Dead a heart made of *hemag* is mentioned, and two such heart-shaped amulets of amethyst are preserved in the Boulaq Museum. As the amethyst retained its repute as a stone of beauty and power through the Greek and Roman periods, we may safely assert that it was set in both the first and second breastplates. Upon the *aḥlamah* was engraved the name Dan.

X. Tarshish. [תַּרְשִׁישׁ] The Septuagint renders this word "chrysolite," where it is used in the description of the breastplate, as does Josephus also. In the Authorized Version, "beryl" is the rendering. We have already stated that the topaz of the ancients was usually our chrysolite, or peridot, and the name "chrysolite" appears to have been used to designate our topaz. This is indeed indicated by the literal meaning of the word, "golden-stone." The *tarshish* received its name from Tartessus, in Spain, an important commercial station of the Phœnicians. The stone derived from this source was not, of course, our Oriental topaz, a variety of corundum, nor was it the true topaz; neither is it at all likely that the name *tarshish* signified, at least originally, the genuine topaz; most probably it denoted a variety of quartz which occurs in Spain. This is originally black, but is decolorized by heating to a deep brown, and if the heating be prolonged the stone becomes paler and eventually entirely transparent. The ancients were familiar with this property. In ancient Egyptian records a stone called *thehen* is frequently mentioned as a material from which amulets were made. This Egyptian name signified primarily a "yellow stone," and might designate either the topaz or the yellow jasper, known and used in Egypt at a very early date; the topaz was probably not known there earlier than 500 or 600 B.C. Hence, in spite of the unquestionable difficulty offered by the geographical name *tarshish,* which might seem to confine us to a Spanish origin for the stone, the probabilities favor the selection of the yellow jasper as the tenth gem in Aaron's breastplate. For that made with pious zeal by those who labored to renew the glories of the Old Jerusalem, we choose the topaz,—possibly, indeed, a fine specimen of the genuine topaz,—for whatever the quality of the yellow stone originally brought from Tartessus, the name may well have been applied to the genuine topaz when that stone became known to the Jews, either in Babylonia, or after their return to Palestine. The *tarshish* was engraved with the name Naphtali.

XI. Shoham. [שֹׁהַם] The Septuagint translates "beryl," but in our Authorized Version and in that used by Roman Catholics, the so-called Douai Version, the word is invariably rendered "onyx." Diodorus Siculus and Dionysius Periegetes, writing in the first century B.C., are the first classical authors who use the name beryl.

While this name does not appear in the treatise of Theophrastus, he evidently includes the beryl among his *smaragdi;* indeed, the true emerald is simply a variety of the beryl, and owes its beautiful coloration to a slight admixture of chromium. The finest beryls were brought from India. Besides the specimen set in the breastplate, the high-priest wore on his shoulders two *shoham* stones, each engraved with the names of six of the tribes. After carefully weighing the evidence, we believe that the stones worn by the high-priest of the Second Temple were aquamarines (beryls). In our endeavor to determine the *shoham* stones used in Mosaic times, we have no very definite information to guide us; on the whole, the conjecture of J. L. Myers, that they were malachites, seems to have much in its favor, for this material was known to the ancient Egyptians and appears to have been often used for amulets. The Egyptian name for malachite, as well as for other green stones, was *mafek,* and a ring of *mafek* is mentioned in an Egyptian text; undoubtedly, at a later period in Egyptian history, *mafek* may also have denoted the beryl. In view of the fact that the turquoise was unquestionably known to the Egyptians at a very early date, the supply being derived from mines in the Sinai Peninsula, which were rediscovered by Macdonald, we might be tempted to suggest that the *shoham* stones were turquoises. The light blue or blue-green of the specimens of this stone found on Mt. Sinai would make an even better contrast with the neighboring jade than would the bright green malachite. On the *shoham* of the breastplate the name Gad was engraved.

XII. Yashpheh. [יָשְׁפֵה.] If, as appears almost certain, this name originally occupied the sixth place in the original Hebrew text, all the ancient versions agree in translating it "jasper." An Assyrian form of the name was *yashpu,* as is shown by the Tell el Amarna letters in the cuneiform writing dating from not long before the Exodus. Of all the so-called jaspers none were so highly valued as those of a green color. The talismanic and therapeutic qualities of the "green jaspers" are often noted by ancient writers, and, according to Galen, these stones were recommended for remedial use by Egyptian writers on medicine. Abel Remusat, the great French Orientalist, writing in 1820, was one of the first to see in the *yashpheh* of the Hebrews and in the green jasper of the Greeks and Romans, the material jade (nephrite or jadeite), the Chinese *yu*-stone. These minerals were used both in the Old and the New World, and were everywhere believed to possess wonderful virtues. Very likely the powers supposed to characterize jade were later attributed to green jasper, but there is every reason to suppose that the true jade was always more highly prized than its jasper substitute, for it was much rarer, and was easily distinguishable, by its translucency, from jasper of a similar color. Until quite recently only Turkestan, Burma and New Zealand have supplied jade and most of that used in other lands came from prehistoric relics or from sources unknown to us. It seems highly probable that the *yashpheh* which adorned the breastplate made for Aaron was a piece of nephrite or jadeite; possibly in the later breastplate green jasper may have been employed. This stone was inscribed with the tribal name Assher.

In the following lists of the precious and semiprecious stones contained in the earlier and later breastplates, the writer does not claim to have finally solved the problem presented by the Hebrew accounts of the high-priest's adornment, but he hopes that the distinction established here between the Mosaic breastplate and that of the Second Temple, separated from each other by an interval of eight centuries, may serve to clear up some of the difficulties encountered in the treatment of this subject.

	The Breastplate of Aaron.	The Breastplate of the Second Temple.
I	Red jasper	Carnelian
II	Light-green serpentine	Peridot
III	Green feldspar	Emerald
IV	Almandine garnet	Ruby
V	Lapis-lazuli	Lapis-lazuli
VI	Onyx	Onyx
VII	Brown agate	Sapphire or jacinth
VIII	Banded agate	Banded agate
IX	Amethyst	Amethyst
X	Yellow jasper	Topaz
XI	Malachite	Beryl
XII	Green jasper, or jade	Green jasper, or jade

The following lists show the variations of the different ancient authorities in regard to the names of the gems in the breastplate:

	Hebrew.	Septuagint. (Greek) About 250 B.C.	Josephus (Greek) About 90 A.D.	Vulgate (Latin) About 400 A.D.	Authorized Version 1611 A.D.	Revised Version 1884 A.D.
1	Odem	Sardion	Sardonyx	Sardius	Sardius	Sardius (or Ruby)
2	Pitdah	Topazion	Topazos	Topazius	Topaz	Topaz
3	Bareketh	Smaragdos	Smaragdos	Smaragdus	Carbuncle	Carbuncle (or Emerald)
4	Nophak	Anthrax	Anthrax	Carbunculus	Emerald	Emerald (or Carbuncle)
5	Sappir	Sappheiros	Iaspis	Sapphirius	Sapphire	Sapphire
6	Yahalom	Iaspis	Sappheiros	Jaspis	Diamond	Diamond (or Sardonyx)
7	Leshem	Ligurion	Liguros	Ligurius	Ligure	Jacinth (or Amber)
8	Shebo	Achatês	Amethystos	Achatês	Agate	Agate
9	Ahlamah	Amethystos	Achatês	Amethystus	Amethyst	Amethyst
10	Tarshish	Chrysolithos	Chrysolithos	Chrysolithus	Beryl	Beryl (or Chalcedony)
11	Shoham	Bêryllion	Onyx	Onychinus	Onyx	Onyx (or Beryl)
12	Yashpheh	Onychion	Bêryllos	Bêryllus	Jasper	Jasper

The high-priest's breastplate, as described in Hebrew tradition, was regarded by the Jews with peculiar reverence, and the stones set in it were believed to be emblematic of many things. It is, therefore, quite natural that these stones are described in the book of Revelation as the foundation stones of the New Jerusalem. The names are in some cases not identical with those given in Exodus, but this may arise from various renderings of the Hebrew names in the Targums or in the Greek versions.

The text in Revelation (xxi, 9–21) is as follows:

And there came unto me one of the seven angels which had the seven vials full of the seven last plagues, and talked with me, saying, Come hither, I will show thee the bride, the Lamb's wife:

And he carried me away in the spirit to a great and high mountain, and showed me that great city, the holy Jerusalem, descending out of heaven from God.

Having the glory of God: and her light was like unto a stone most precious, even like a jasper-stone, clear as crystal;

And had a wall great and high, and had twelve gates, and at the gates twelve angels, and names written thereon, which are the names of the twelve tribes of the children of Israel:

On the east, three gates; on the north, three gates; on the south, three gates; and on the west, three gates.

And the wall of the city had twelve foundations, and in them the names of the twelve apostles of the Lamb.

And he that talked with me had a golden reed to measure the city, and the gates thereof, and the wall thereof.

And the city lieth foursquare, and the length is as large as the breadth: and he measured the city with the reed, twelve thousand furlongs. The length and the breadth and the height of it are equal.

And he measured the wall thereof, an hundred and forty and four cubits, according to the measure of a man, that is, of the angel.

And the building of the wall of it was of jasper: and the city was pure gold, like unto clear glass.

And the foundations of the wall of the city were garnished with all manner of precious stones. The first foundation was jasper; the second, sapphire; the third, a chalcedony; the fourth, an emerald;

The fifth, sardonyx; the sixth, sardius; the seventh, chrysolite; the eighth, beryl; the ninth, a topaz; the tenth, a chrysoprasus; the eleventh, a jacinth; the twelfth, an amethyst.

And the twelve gates were twelve pearls; every several gate was of one pearl: and the street of the city was pure gold, as it were transparent glass.

It is easy to trace in this description the substitution of the twelve apostles for the twelve tribes in connection with the precious stones enumerated, and, besides this, we also have the twelve angels, associated at a later date with the months and the signs of the zodiac.

Of the twelve foundation stones the Revelation of St. John expressly states that they had "in them the names of the twelve apostles of the Lamb." The assignment of each stone to the respective apostle was made in later times according to the order given in the lists of the apostles contained in the so-called Synoptic Gospels, Matthew, Mark, and Luke. These lists are not quite identical—Andrew, for instance, being placed second in Matthew and Luke, but fourth in Mark—and the same stone was not always assigned to a given apostle. Frequently the list was modified by the addition of the apostle Paul, really the thirteenth apostle. In this case he was usually given the second place immediately after St. Peter, and to the brothers James and John, the "Sons of Thunder," was assigned a single stone; in some later arrangements St. Paul occupies the last place, after St. Matthias, who was chosen to take the place of Judas Iscariot, and whose name as an apostle first appears in the Acts.

LISTS OF THE APOSTLES.

Gospel of St. Matthew x, 2–4.	Gospel of St. Mark iii, 16–19.	Gospel of St. Luke vi, 14–16.
Peter	Peter	Peter
Andrew	James	Andrew
James	John	James
John	Andrew	John
Philip	Philip	Philip
Bartholomew	Bartholomew	Bartholomew
Thomas	Matthew	Matthew
Matthew	Thomas	Thomas
James the Less	James the Less	James the Less
Thaddeus	Thaddeus	Simon Zelotes
Simon Zelotes	Simon Zelotes	Judas
Judas Iscariot	Judas Iscariot	Judas Iscariot

The passage in Revelation xxi, 19, 20, is not the only one in that book treating of precious stones, for we read in chapter iv, 2, 3:

And immediately I was in the Spirit: and, behold, a throne was set in heaven, and *one* sat on the throne.

And he that sat was to look upon like a jasper and a sardine stone: and *there was* a rainbow round about the throne, in sight like unto an emerald.

The commentators, both ancient and modern, have given many different explanations of the symbolic meaning of the similes employed here. Some have seen in the two stones a type of the two judgments of the world, by fire and by water; others find that they signify the holiness of God and his justice. Of the rainbow "like unto an emerald," Alford says we should not think it strange that the bow is green, instead of prismatic: "the *form* is that of the covenant bow, the color even more refreshing and more directly symbolizing grace and mercy." [16]

---

[16] Alford, "The Greek Testament," vol. iv, Pt. 2, p. 594.

The significance of the twelve Apocalyptic gems is given by Rabanus Maurus, Archbishop of Mainz (786–856), in the following words: [17]

In the jasper is figured the truth of faith; in the sapphire, the height of celestial hope; in the chalcedony, the flame of inner charity. In the emerald is expressed the strength of faith in adversity; in the sardonyx, the humility of the saints in spite of their virtues; in the sard, the venerable blood of the martyrs. In the chrysolite, indeed, is shown true spiritual preaching accompanied by miracles; in the beryl, the perfect operation of prophecy; in the topaz, the ardent contemplation of the prophecies. Lastly, in the chrysoprase is demonstrated the work of the blessed martyrs and their reward; in the hyacinth, the celestial rapture of the learned in their high thoughts and their humble descent to human things out of regard for the weak; in the amethyst, the constant thought of the heavenly kingdom in humble souls.

The origin of the foundation stones named in Revelation xxi, 19, 20, may be found in the text, Isaiah liv, 11, 12, where we read:

O thou afflicted, tossed with tempest, *and* not comforted, behold, I will lay thy stones with fair colours, and lay thy foundations with sapphires.

And I will make thy windows of agates, and thy gates of carbuncles, and all thy borders of pleasant stones.

As we see, only three stones are mentioned by name: the sapphire, the carbuncle, and "agates." This last rendering is quite doubtful, as the Hebrew word (*kodkodim*) signifies shining or gleaming stones, and their use for windows indicates that they must have been transparent. It is easy to understand that in later times the twelve stones of the breastplate, dedicated to the twelve tribes of Israel, were used to fill out and com-

[17] Rabani Mauri, "Opera Omnia," vol. v, col. 470. Patrologiæ Lat., vol. cxi, Parisiis, 1864.

plete the picture, following the indication given by the general terms "stones with fair colours" and "pleasant stones."

In commenting on this text Rabbi Johanan is quoted in the Babylonian Talmud as saying that God would bring jewels and pearls thirty ells square (twenty ells in height and ten in width) and would place them on the gates of Jerusalem. There may be in this some reminiscence of the Apocalyptic foundation stones. A sceptical disciple said to the Rabbi, "We do not ever find a jewel as large as the egg of a dove." But not long afterward, when this same disciple was sailing in a boat on the sea, he saw angels sawing stones as immense as those described by Rabbi Johanan, and when he asked for what they were designed, the reply was, "The Holy One, blessed be He, will place them on the gates of Jerusalem." [18]

---

[18] "New Edition of the Babylonian Talmud," ed. and trans. by Michael L. Rodkinson, vol. v (xiii), New York, 1902, p. 210. Baba Batra.

III

Birth-Stones

THE origin of the belief that to each month of the year a special stone was dedicated, and that the stone of the month was endowed with a peculiar virtue for those born in that month and was their natal stone, may be traced back to the writings of Josephus, in the first century of our era, and to those of St. Jerome, in the early part of the fifth century. Both these authors distinctly proclaim the connection between the twelve stones of the high-priest's breastplate and the twelve months of the year, as well as the twelve zodiacal signs. Strange to say, however, in spite of this early testimony, we have no instance of the usage of wearing such stones as natal stones until a comparatively late date; indeed, it appears that this custom originated in Poland some time during the eighteenth century. The reason for this seems to have been that the virtues attributed to each particular stone, more especially the therapeutic virtues, rendered it necessary to recommend the wearing of one or the other, according to the disease from which the person was suffering, for his natal stone might not have the power to cure his particular ailment, or might not bring about the fulfilment of his dearest wish. In other words, the belief in the special virtues of the stone was paramount, and it was long before the mystic bond between the stone of the month and the person born in that month was fully realized.

The order in which the foundation stones of the New Jerusalem are given in the book of Revelation determined the succssion of natal stones for the months. The first stone was assigned to St. Peter and to the month of March, to the leader of the apostles and to the month of the spring equinox; the second to the month of April; the third to May, etc. When, however, many centuries later,—probably in Poland, as we have stated,—with the aid of the rabbis or the Hebrew gem traders, the wearing of natal stones became usual, certain changes had been made in this order and some stones not mentioned among those of the breastplate, or of the New Jerusalem, were substituted for certain of these,—notably the turquoise for the month of December, the ruby for July, and the diamond for April. In modern times the turquoise has become the stone for July while the ruby has been assigned to December.

There is some evidence in favor of the theory that at the outset all twelve stones were acquired by the same person and worn in turn, each one during the respective month to which it was assigned, or during the ascendancy of its zodiacal sign. The stone of the month was believed to exercise its therapeutic or talismanic virtue to the fullest extent at that period. Perhaps the fact that this entailed a monthly change of ornaments may rather have been a recommendation of the usage than the reverse.[1]

It seems highly probable that the development of the belief in natal stones that took place in Poland was due to the influence of the Jews who settled in that country shortly before we have historic notice of the use of the twelve stones for those born in the respective months. The lively interest always felt by the Jews regarding the gems of the breastplate, the many and various commen-

[1] Brückmann, "Abhandlung von Edelsteinen," 2d ed., Braunschweig, 1773, p. 358.

taries their learned men have written upon this subject, and the fact that the well-to-do among the chosen people have always carried with them in their wanderings many precious stones, all this seems to make it likely that to the Jews should be attributed the fashion of wearing natal stones.

However, whether this conjecture be correct or erroneous, the fashion once started became soon quite general and has as many votaries to-day as ever before. There can be no doubt that the owner of a ring or ornament set with a natal stone is impressed with the idea of possessing something more intimately associated with his or her personality than any other stone, however beautiful or costly it may be. If it be objected that this is nothing but imagination due to sentiment, we must bear in mind that imagination is one of the most potent factors in our life; indeed, the great Napoleon is quoted as saying that it ruled the world.

Probably the very earliest text we have in which the stones of the breastplate are positively associated with the months of the year is to be found in the "Antiquities of the Jews," by Flavius Josephus.[2] This runs as follows:

> Moreover, the vestments of the high-priest being made of linen signifies the earth, the blue denotes the sky, being like lightning in its pomegranates, and resembling thunder in the noise of the bells. And as for the ephod, it showed that God had made the universe of four elements, and as for the gold interwoven in it, I suppose it related to the splendor by which all things are to be enlightened. He also appointed the breastplate to be placed in the middle of the ephod to resemble the earth, for that occupies the middle place in the world; and the girdle,

---

[2] Flavii Josephi, ed. Dindorf, Parisii, 1847, vol. ii, p. 97; "Antiq. Jud," lib. iii, cap. 7, paragraph 7. In the second century, Clemens Alexandrinus (lib. v, cap. 6) repeats this idea of Josephus, adding that the four rows in which the gems were disposed signified the four seasons of the year.

which encompassed the high priest about, signifies the ocean, for that goes about everything. And the two sardonyxes that were in the clasps on the high-priest's shoulders, indicate to us the sun and the moon. And for the twelve stones, whether we understand by them the months, or the twelve signs of what the Greeks call the zodiac, we shall not be mistaken in their meaning. And for the cap, which was of a blue color, it seems to me to mean heaven, for otherwise the name of God would not have been inscribed upon it. That it was also adorned with a crown, and that of gold also, is because of the splendor with which God is pleased.

This passage was adapted by St. Jerome, three hundred years later, in his letter to Fabiola,[3] and undoubtedly laid the foundation for the later custom of wearing one of these stones as a natal or birth-stone for a person born in a given month, or for an astral or zodiacal stone for one born under a given zodiacal sign. As we see, both uses are indicated by the passage of Josephus. In the later centuries, as the book of Revelation, which was generally less favored at the outset than the other parts of the New Testament, became a subject of devout study, and a mine of mystical suggestions, the twelve foundation stones (Rev. xxi, 19) of the New Jerusalem largely took the place of the stones of the breastplate. While this list of foundation stones is unquestionably based upon the much earlier list of the stones adorning Aaron's breastplate, the ordering differs considerably and there are some changes in the material; possibly many, if not all, of these differences may be due to textual errors or to a transcription from memory.

That the foundation stones were inscribed with the names of the apostles is expressly stated (Rev. xxi, 14), but it was not until the eighth or ninth century that the commentators on Revelation busied themselves with

[3] Sancti Hieronymi, "Opera Omnia," ed. Migne, Parisiis, 1877, vol. i, col. 616; Epistola lxiv, paragraph 16.

finding analogies between these stones and the apostles. At the outset, the symbolism of the stones was looked upon from a purely religious standpoint. Few of the early fathers—we may except Epiphanius—thought or cared much for the stones themselves, or knew much of them; but, in time, their natural beauty became more and more highly developed as the lapidarian art demanded better cut and choicer material, their supposed virtues came to the fore, and the symbolism was strengthened and emphasized by a reference to their innate qualities and also to their peculiar powers. The fact that this part of the tradition was rather of pagan than of Christian origin probably contributed to render it less attractive to the early Christians, so that it was not until Christianity had become practically universal in the Greek and Roman world and the opposition to pagan traditions, as such, was weakened and, indeed, largely forgotten, that the virtues of the stones were made prominent, and certain parts of these superstitions were retained, as were some of the pagan ceremonies in the Christian religion.

One of the earliest writers to associate directly with the apostles the symbolism of the gems given as foundation stones of the New Jerusalem by St. John in Revelation xxi, 19, is Andreas, bishop of Cæsarea. This author was at one time assigned by critics to the fifth century A.D.,[4] but more recent investigation has shown that he probably belonged to the last half of the tenth century. His exposition reads as follows:[5]

The jasper, which like the emerald is of a greenish hue, probably signifies St. Peter, chief of the apostles, as one who so bore Christ's death in his inmost nature that his love for Him was always vigorous

[4] Lücke, "Versuch einer Einleitung in die Offenbarung Johannes," Bonn, 1852, p. 964.

[5] Patrologiæ Græcæ, ed. Migne, vol. cvi, Parisiis, 1863, cols. 433–438.

and fresh. By his fervent faith he has become our shepherd and leader.

As the sapphire is likened to the heavens (from this stone is made a color popularly called lazur), I conceive it to mean St. Paul, since he was caught up to the third heaven, where his soul was firmly fixed. Thither he seeks to draw all those who may be obedient to him.

The chalcedony was not inserted in the high-priest's breastplate, but instead the carbuncle, of which no mention is made here. It may well be, however, that the author designated the carbuncle by the name chalcedony. Andrew, then, can be likened to the carbuncle, since he was splendidly illumined by the fire of the Spirit.

The emerald, which is of a green color, is nourished with oil, that its transparency and beauty may not change; we conceive this stone to signify John the Evangelist. He, indeed, soothed the souls dejected by sin with a divine oil, and by the grace of his excellent doctrine lends constant strength to our faith.

By the sardonyx, showing with a certain transparency and purity the color of the human nail, we believe that James is denoted, seeing that he bore death for Christ before all others. This the nail by its color indicates, for it may be cut off without any sensible pain.

The sardius with its tawny and translucent coloring suggests fire, and it possesses the virtue of healing tumors and wounds inflicted by iron; hence I consider that it designates the beauty of virtue characterizing the apostle Philip, for his virtue, animated by the fire of the Holy Spirit, cured the soul of the wounds inflicted by the wiles of the devil, and revived it.

The chrysolite, gleaming with the splendor of gold, may symbolize Bartholomew, since he was illustrious for his divine preaching and his store of virtues.

The beryl, imitating the colors of the sea and of the air, and not unlike the jacinth, seems to suggest the admirable Thomas, especially as he made a long journey by sea, and even reached the Indies, sent by God to preach salvation to the peoples of that region.

The topaz, which is of a ruddy color, resembling somewhat the carbuncle, stops the discharge of the milky fluid with which those having eye-disease suffer. This seems to denote Matthew, for he was animated by a divine zeal, and, his blood being fired because of Christ, he was found worthy to enlighten by his Gospel those whose heart was blinded, that they might like new-born children drink of the milk of the faith.

The chrysoprase, more brightly tinged with a golden hue than

FACSIMILE OF THE BETROTHAL RING OF THE VIRGIN IN THE CATHEDRAL OF PERUGIA.

The original ring, which is of chalcedony, is shown on St. Agatha's Day, July 29, to cure ailments of mothers. This cord and facsimile of ring acquired by the author at Perugia, May 6, 1902.

gold itself, symbolizes St. Thaddæus; the gold (*chrysos*) symbolizing the kingdom of Christ, and the *prassius,* Christ's death, both of which he preached to Abgar, King of Edessa.

The jacinth, which is of a celestial hue, signifies Simon Zelotes, zealous for the gifts and grace of Christ and endowed with a celestial prudence.

By the amethyst, which shows to the onlooker a fiery aspect, is signified Matthias, who in the gift of tongues was so filled with celestial fire and with fervent zeal to serve and please God, who had chosen him, that he was found worthy to take the place of the apostate Judas.

Some theologians were opposed to the assignment of the foundation stones to the apostles, for they held that only Christ himself could be regarded as the foundation of his Church. Hence the symbolism of these stones was made to apply to Christ alone, the color of the stone often guiding the commentator in his choice of ideas denoted by the different gems. Thus, one writer, applying all the meanings to Christ, finds that the greenish Jasper denotes satisfaction; the sky-blue Sapphire, the soul; the bright-red Chalcedony, zeal for truth; the transparent green Emerald, kindness and goodness; the nail-colored Sardonyx, the strength of spiritual life; the red Sardius, readiness to shed His blood for the Church; the yellow Chrysolite, the excellence of His divine nature; the sea-green Beryl, moderation and the control of the passions; the glass-green Topaz (chrysolite?), uprightness; the harsh-colored Chrysoprase, sternness towards sinners; the violet or purple Jacinth, royal dignity, and, lastly, the purple Amethyst, with a touch of red, perfection.[6]

Andreas of Cæsarea freely recognizes his indebtedness to the much more ancient source, St. Epiphanius, bishop of Constantia in Cyprus, who died in 402 A.D., and who wrote a short but very valuable treatise on the

---

[6] Georgius Vitringa, "Nauwkeurige onderzoek van de goddelyke Openbaring der H. Apostels Johannes," Dutch trans. of Latin by M. Gargon, Amsterdam, 1728, vol. ii, p. 681.

stones of the breastplate, noting in several cases the therapeutic and talismanic virtues of these stones and giving his opinion as to the order in which the names of the tribes were inscribed upon them.[7] As the foundation stones of Revelation are rightly called "apostolic stones," so those of the breastplate merit the designation of "tribal stones," as well as that of astral stones; indeed, the Jews of medieval times definitely associated the tribes with the zodiacal signs in the following order:

Judah	Aries
Issachar	Taurus
Zebulun	Gemini
Reuben	Cancer
Simeon	Leo
Gad	Virgo
Ephraim	Libra
Manasseh	Scorpio
Benjamin	Sagittarius
Dan	Capricorn
Naphtali	Aquarius
Asher	Pisces

For Rabanus Maurus the nine gems of the king of Tyre named in Ezekiel xxxviii, 13, are types of the nine orders of angels, just as the twelve foundation stones of Revelation signify the twelve apostles.[8]

It is evident, from early and later usage, that, at the place and time where and when these stones were first utilized for birth-stones, the year must have begun with the month of March. This will be apparent when we compare the following eight lists, carefully gathered from various sources:

[7] Sancti Patris Epiphanii episcopi Cypri ad Diodorum Tyri episcopum, "De XII. Gemmis, quæ erant in veste Aaronis," ed. Gesner, Tiguri, 1565.

[8] Rabani Mauri, "Opera Omnia," vol. v, col. 465; in Patrologiæ Latinæ, ed. Migne, vol. xvi, Paris, 1864.

Month	Jews	Romans	Isidore Bishop of Seville	Arabians	Poles	Russians	Italians	15th to 20th Century
January	Garnet	Garnet	Hyacinth	Garnet	Garnet	Garnet Hyacinth	Jacinth Garnet	Garnet
February	Amethyst	Amethyst	Amethyst	Amethyst	Amethyst	Amethyst	Amethyst	Amethyst Hyacinth Pearl
March	Jasper	Bloodstone	Jasper	Bloodstone	Bloodstone	Jasper	Jasper	Jasper Bloodstone
April	Sapphire	Sapphire	Sapphire	Sapphire	Diamond	Sapphire	Sapphire	Diamond Sapphire
May	Chalcedony Carnelian Agate	Agate	Agate	Emerald	Emerald	Emerald	Agate	Emerald Agate
June	Emerald	Emerald	Emerald	Agate Chalcedony Pearl	Agate Chalcedony	Agate Chalcedony	Emerald	Cat's-eye Turquoise Agate
July	Onyx	Onyx	Onyx	Carnelian	Ruby	Ruby Sardonyx	Onyx	Turquoise Onyx
August	Carnelian	Carnelian	Carnelian	Sardonyx	Sardonyx	Alexandrite	Carnelian	Sardonyx Carnelian Moonstone Topaz
September	Chrysolite	Sardonyx	Chrysolite	Chrysolite	Sardonyx	Chrysolite	Chrysolite	Chrysolite
October	Aquamarine	Aquamarine	Aquamarine	Aquamarine	Aquamarine	Beryl	Beryl	Beryl Opal
November	Topaz	Topaz	Topaz	Topaz	Topaz	Topaz	Topaz	Topaz Pearl
December	Ruby	Ruby	Ruby	Ruby	Turquoise	Turquoise Chrysoprase	Ruby	Ruby Bloodstone

It may be interesting to show in these eight lists the stones which are most favored in each month in the following way, the numerals indicating the number of lists in which the stones appear (including the alternate stones):

January..... Garnet 7, hyacinth 2.
February.... Amethyst 8, hyacinth 1, pearl 1.
March....... Jasper 5, bloodstone 4.
April........ Sapphire 7, diamond 2.
May.......... Agate 5, emerald 4, chalcedony 1, carnelian 1.
June .... Emerald 4, agate 4, chalcedony 3, turquoise 1, pearl 1, cat's-eye 1.
July.......... Onyx 5, sardonyx 1, carnelian 1, ruby 1, turquoise 1.
August ...... Carnelian 5, sardonyx 3, moonstone 1, topaz 1, alexandrite 1.
September ... Chrysolite 6, sardonyx 2.
October...... Beryl, 8, aquamarine 5, opal 1.
November ... Topaz 8, pearl 1.
December.... Ruby 6, turquoise 2, chrysoprase 1, bloodstone 1.

With the exception of January, where we have the garnet instead of the jacinth, and of December, which gives us the ruby instead of the chrysoprase, the first choices are practically identical with the foundation stones, bearing in mind that the eleventh stone is that for January, the twelfth that for February, the first that for March and so on.

Of the assignment of the natal stones to the different months of the year or to the zodiacal signs, Poujet fils, writing in 1762, states that in his opinion this fashion started in Germany—others say in Poland—some two centuries before his time, and he adds that, though this arrangement was purely imaginary, and unknown to ancient writers, it soon became popular, and many, more especially of the fair sex, seeing in it an element of mystery, wished to wear rings set with the stone appropriate to the month of their birth, the stone being engraved with the appropriate zodiacal sign.[9] However correct Poujet may be regarding the period at which the fashion of wearing natal rings was introduced, he is, as we have already shown, quite wrong in believing that the serial arrangement of the stones and their assignment to months or signs was purely imaginary, for it is unquestionably based on the list in Revelation, which in its turn goes back to the twelve stones of the high-priest's breastplate.

The fashion of wearing a series of twelve stones denoting (or bearing) the zodiacal signs seems to have existed in the sixteenth century, for Catherine de' Medici is said to have worn a girdle set with twelve stones, among which were certain onyxes as large as crown-pieces, upon which talismanic designs had been engraved. Two hundred years later this girdle is stated to have been in the possession of a M. d'Ennery, whose collection of antique medals was regarded as the finest in Paris at the time.[10] It is not, however, certain that the twelve stones of Catherine's girdle were those attributed to the zodiacal signs both at an earlier and later period.

Though the substitution of a new schedule for the time-honored list of birth-stones has received the approval of the National Association of Jewellers at the meeting in Kansas City August, 1912, it can scarcely be said to offer a satisfactory solution of the question, which has its importance not only from a commercial point of view, but also because the idea that birth-stones possess a certain indefinable, but none the less real significance, has long been present and still exercises a spell over the

---

[9] Poujet fils, "Traité des pierres précieuses," Paris, 1762, p. 4.

[10] Poujet fils, l.c.

minds of all who are gifted with a touch of imagination, or romance, if you will. The longing for something that appeals to this sense is much more general than is commonly supposed, and is a not unnatural reaction against the progress of materialism, against the assertion that there is nothing in heaven or earth but what we can definitely apprehend through our senses.

It is this persuasion that should be chiefly considered in any attempt to tamper with the traditional attribution of the stones to particular months or to the zodiacal signs. Once we allow the spirit of commercialism pure and simple to dictate the choice of such stones, according to the momentary interest of dealers, there is grave danger that the only true incentive to acquire birth-stones will be weakened and people will lose interest in them. Sentiment, true sentiment, is one of the best things in human nature. While if darkened by fear it may lead to pessimism, with all the evils which such a state of mind implies, if illumined by hope it gives to humanity a brighter forecast of the future, an optimism that helps people over difficult passages in their lives. Thus, sentiment must not be neglected, and nothing is more likely to destroy it than the conviction that it is being constantly exploited for purposes of commercialism. For this reason, the interest as well as the inclination of all who are concerned in this question of birth-stones should induce a very careful handling of the subject.

Quite true it is that there are now, and have been in the past, several lists of these stones, differing slightly from one another, but all are based essentially either upon the list of foundation stones given in Revelation (xxi, 19) or upon that of the gems adorning the breastplate of Aaron and enumerated in Exodus (xxxix, 10–13). For convenient reference, we give the latter according to the Authorized Version of the Scriptures, and also as corrected by later research, and the former according to the Authorized Version.

	Breastplate. Authorized Version.	Breastplate. Later Correction.	Foundation Stones. Authorized Version.
I	Sardius	Carnelian	Jasper
II	Topaz	Chrysolite (peridot)	Sapphire
III	Carbuncle	Emerald	Chalcedony
IV	Emerald	Ruby	Emerald
V	Sapphire	Lapis-lazuli	Sardonyx
VI	Diamond	Onyx	Sardius
VII	Ligure	Sapphire	Chrysolite
VIII	Agate	Agate	Beryl
IX	Amethyst	Amethyst	Topaz
X	Beryl	Topaz	Chrysoprasus
XI	Onyx	Beryl	Jacinth
XII	Jasper	Jasper	Amethyst

While the arrangement differs in Revelation, the stones are nearly identical. For chalcedonius, we should probably read *carchedonius,* a name of the ruby; sardonyx is the onyx of Exodus; the jacinth (sapphire) is probably the "ligure"; the sapphire was the lapis-lazuli, and sardius is equivalent to carnelian. There thus remains only the chrysoprase, which for some reason has substituted the agate. In the eventual association of the foundation stones with the months, the first, the jasper, was assigned to March, with which month the year was reckoned to begin.

The list suggested and adopted in Kansas City reads as follows:

Month.	Birth-stone.	Alternate Stone.
January	Garnet	
February	Amethyst	
March	Bloodstone	Aquamarine
April	Diamond	
May	Emerald	
June	Pearl	Moonstone
July	Ruby	

Month.	Birth-stone.	Alternate-stone.
August	Sardonyx	Peridot
September	Sapphire	
October	Opal	Tourmaline
November	Topaz	
December	Turquoise	Lapis-lazuli

Among the many changes in this list from that habitually followed, it will be noted that the ruby is transferred from December to July, changing places with the turquoise, which became the gem of December. This has been favored on the ground that the warmer-colored gem was best adapted for a July birth-stone, while the paler turquoise was best suited to a winter month, when the sun's rays are feeble. The contrary, however, is true; for it is in winter that we seek for warmth, while in the heat of summer nothing is more grateful than coolness. This transposition is, in effect, simply a return to the ordering of these stones in the Polish list, which may perhaps have become popular in Europe in the eighteenth century through Marie Leczinska, the queen of Louis XV. Another undesirable change takes the chrysolite (peridot) from the place it has always occupied as the gem of September, and makes of it an alternate for August, with the sardonyx, while the sapphire, properly the gem for April, is made the birth-stone for September. For October neither the tourmaline nor the opal is as appropriate as the beryl, while for June we should prefer the asteria to the moonstone as a substitute for the pearl.

This suggested radical change or violation cannot be permitted. The time-honored ordering is familiar now to all who are interested in the matter, and any change, even if one apparently for the better, is liable to disturb the popular confidence in those who are supposed to be familiar with the subject. Above all, there should be no duplication or triplication of birth-stones for any given month, the choice between a birth-stone or an astral or zodiacal stone or the combination of these affording all the variety that is necessary or should be desired.

As the diamond does not appear to have been known to the ancients and is not given in any of the lists of birth-stones before the last century, and as diamonds, like gold and platinum, may easily be used as accessories to other stones, would it not perhaps be better to omit the diamond from the list of the stones of the months, and rather use these gems as a bordering or other ornate addition to the stone of the month? The pearl, which is not a stone in any sense of the word, should not appear in the list at all; but it can be worn in some device suggesting a sentiment, as, for instance, an emblem of purity, etc.

The tourmaline, as a gem only known in modern times or since the eighteenth century, seems out of place in the list of birth-stones, which ought only to comprise precious or semi-precious stones which have been known and worn from ancient times.

"Astral stones" or "zodiacal stones" are terms used to designate those gems which were believed to be peculiarly and mystically related to the zodiacal signs. While these signs constitute a twelve-fold division of the year just as do the months, they do not exactly coincide with the latter as now reckoned, but overlap them, so that the sign Aquarius, for instance, covers the period from January 21 to February 20, that of Pisces from February 21 to March 20, that of Aries, the spring sign, from March 21 to April 20, and so on down to Capricornus, which begins at the winter solstice. Thus, every necessary opportunity is afforded for enlarging the selection of natal stones while preserving the traditional order of those appropriate to the months, an order which in its origin dates back to the early Christian centuries and which, from the close relation with the sacred gems of the Scriptures, it seems almost sacrilegious to violate by arbitrary changes.

CARNELIAN, ENGRAVED WITH THE ZODIACAL SIGNS, TAURUS, LEO AND CAPRICORN; IN THE CENTRE A SIX-RAYED STAR, THE FORM OF ONE OF THESE RAYS DENOTING A COMET. (See p. 341.)

Referred to the nativity of Augustus and to a comet which appeared shortly after the assassination of Julius Cæsar. From De Mairan's "Lettres au R. P. Parrenin," Paris, 1770, opp. p. 274.

Then, in addition, we have the "talismanic gems," or the stones of the twelve guardian angels, one set over all those born in each month. Here we have another time-honored list, differing from either of those mentioned above, so that, in almost if not quite every case, each person has the choice between three different stones as "birth-stones," or can have them combined in an artistic jewel so as to profit by all the favorable influences promised by the old authorities. Thus, there is absolutely no excuse for playing fast and loose with the ancient, popular, and quasi-religious belief in the special virtue of *one particular stone* for each month, and that one the gem long prescribed by usage.

As it might seem appropriate that one born in the United States should wear a gem from among these which our country furnishes, the following list was some time since prepared by the writer, not in any sense as a substitute for the real birth-stones, but as possible accessory gems (when they were not identical), gems which might be worn from a spirit of patriotism. Of course where the stone in question is really that traditionally recommended, the fact that it is at the same time an American gem-stone is an added argument in its favor.

Month.	Stones.	Where found.
January...	Garnet, rhodolite	Montana, New Mexico, Arizona, North Carolina
February..	Amethyst	North Carolina, Georgia, Virginia
March.....	Californite	California
April......	Sapphire	Montana, Idaho
May.......	Green tourmaline	Lake Superior
June......	Moss-agate	California, Montana, Wyoming, Arizona
July.......	Turquoise	New Mexico, California, Arizona
August....	Golden beryl	California, Connecticut, North Carolina
September.	Kunzite	California
October....	Aquamarine	North Carolina, Maine, California
November..	Topaz	Utah, California, Maine
December..	Rubellite	Montana

The year is divided into four seasons or cycles,—spring, summer, fall, and winter,—and each season has its particular gem. The emerald is the gem of the spring, the ruby the gem of summer, the sapphire the gem of autumn, and the diamond the gem of winter.

For spring, no precious stone is more appropriate an the emerald. Its beautiful color is that of Nature, r Nature clothes herself with green when she awakens rom her long rest of winter. Having decked herself vith green of the various tints and colors, she has se- cted a background by which a contrast is made for the wers that come in the spring and summer and ripen into fruit and seeds of autumn. To be a seasonable gem t must be rare, and the emerald is rare. Whether found the mines of Bogotá, whether mined in ancient times at Zabarah in Egypt, or in the past century in the Ural Mountains, it has never been found in abundance. It is softer in color than the ruby and less hard in structure.

The ruby, although as a natal stone it belongs to December, is the gem of summer. It is born in the hot climates,—the pigeon's-blood ruby in Burma, the pomegranate-red in Ceylon, and the more garnet-hued type in Siam,—these three equatorial countries produce the ruby. Those of large size are always rare, and this is the gem which Job valued more highly than any other, although "garnet" may perhaps be a better rendering. It is on an equal plane in hardness, in composition, in crystalline structure, and in every way, with the sapphire. These are sister gems, structurally alike, yet varying in complexion, due to a slight difference which some scientists think is not even dependent upon the coloring matter.

The sapphire—the gem of autumn, the blue of the utumn sky—is a symbol of truth, sincerity, and con- tancy. Less vivid than its sister gem, the ruby, it typi- ies calm and tried affection, not ardent passion; it is therefore appropriate to the autumn season, when the declining sun no longer sends forth the fiery rays of summer but shines with a tempered brilliancy.

The diamond, the gem of winter, typifying the sun, is the gem of light. Its color is that of ice, and as the dewdrop or the drop of water from a mountain stream sparkles in the light of the sun, as the icicle sparkles in winter, and the stars on a cold winter night, so the diamond sparkles, and it combines and contrasts with all known gems. Like light, it illumines them just as the sun does the plants of the earth. The diamond, the gem of light, like light itself when broken into a spectrum, gives us all known colors, and by combining all these colors it gives us white. Like gold, the diamond was made rare, so that it must be searched for, and the mines and deposits contain less of these two substances in a given area than of any other known materials. It is thirty to a hundred times more rare than gold, for if gold occurs one part in 250,000, it can scarcely be worked with profit, while the diamond can be worked to advantage when found only one part in 10,000,000,—yes, even one part in 25,000,000—and, like gold, it sometimes spurs the searcher on to wealth or to ruin. As great nuggets of gold have occasionally been found, so has a diamond been discovered large enough to make the greatest ruler pause to pay its price, and one which it took an entire country to give to that ruler who sways his sceptre over countries in which the world's greatest diamonds have been found.

When the God of the Mines called his courtiers to bring him all known gems, he found them to be of all colors and tints, and of varying hardnesses, such as the ruby, emerald, sapphire, etc., etc. He took one of each; he crushed them; he compounded them, and said: "Let this be something that will combine the beauty of all; yet it must be pure, and it must be invincible." He spoke: and lo! the diamond was born, pure as the dewdrop and invincible in hardness; but when its ray is resolved in the spectrum, it displays all the colors of the gems from which it was made. "Mine," said the god, "must be the gem of the universe; for my queen I will create one that shall be the greatest gem of the sea," and for her he created the pearl.

Gems of Spring	Gems of Summer
Amethyst	Zircon
Green diamond	Garnet (demantoid and ouvarite)
Chrysoberyl	Chrysoberyl (alexandrite)
Spinel (rubicelle)	Spinel
Pink topaz	Pink topaz
Olivine (peridot)	Ruby
Emerald	Fire opal

Gems of Autumn	Gems of Winter
Hyacinth	Diamond
Topaz	Rock-crystal
Sapphire	White sapphire
Jacinth	Turquoise
Cairngorm	Quartz
Adamantine spar	Moonstone
Tourmaline	Pearl
Oriental chrysolite	Labradorite

SENTIMENTS OF THE MONTHS

JANUARY

Natal stone .... Garnet.
Guardian angel .... Gabriel.
His talismanic gem .... Onyx
Special apostle .... Simon Peter.
His gem .... Jasper.
Zodiacal sign .... Aquarius.
Flower .... Snowdrop.

No gems save garnets should be worn
By her who in this month is born;
They will insure her constancy,
True friendship and fidelity.

The gleaming garnet holds within its sway
Faith, constancy, and truth to one alway.

FEBRUARY

Natal stone ....Amethyst.
Guardian angel ....Barchiel.
His talismanic gem ....Jasper.
Special apostle ....Andrew.
His gem ....Carbuncle.
Zodiacal sign ....Pisces.
Flower ....Primrose.

The February-born may find
Sincerity and peace of mind,
Freedom from passion and from care,
If she an amethyst will wear.

Let her an amethyst but cherish well,
And strife and care can never with her dwell.

MARCH

Natal stone ....Jasper, bloodstone.
Guardian Angel ....Malchediel.
His talismanic gem ....Ruby.
Special apostles ....James and John.
Their gem ....Emerald.
Zodiacal sign ....Aries.
Flower ....Ipomœa, violet.

Who on this world of ours her eyes
In March first opens may be wise,
In days of peril firm and brave,
Wears she a bloodstone to her grave.

Who wears a jasper, be life short or long,
Will meet all dangers brave and wise and strong.

APRIL

Natal stone ....Diamond, sapphire.
Guardian angel ....Ashmodei.
His talismanic gem ....Topaz.
Special apostle ....Philip.
His gem ....Carnelian.
Zodiacal sign ....Taurus.
Flower ....Daisy.

She who from April dates her years
Diamonds should wear, lest bitter tears
For vain repentance flow. This stone
Emblem of innocence is known.

Innocence, repentance—sun and shower—
The diamond or the sapphire is her dower.

MAY

Natal stone ....Emerald.
Guardian angel ....Amriel.
His talismanic gem ....Carbuncle.
Special apostle ....Bartholomew.
His gem ....Chrysolite.
Zodiacal sign ....Gemini.
Flower ....Hawthorn.

Who first beholds the light of day
In spring's sweet flow'ry month of May,
And wears an emerald all her life,
Shall be a loved and happy wife.

No happier wife and mother in the land
Than she with emerald shining on her hand.

JUNE

Natal stone ....Agate.
Guardian angel ....Muriel.
His talismanic gem ....Emerald.
Special apostle ....Thomas.
His gem ....Beryl.
Zodiacal sign ....Cancer.
Flower ....Honeysuckle.

1. Moss agate mocha stone, Hindoostan.
2. Moss agate, Brazil, S. A.

Who comes with summer to this earth,
And owes to June her hour of birth,
With ring of agate on her hand
Can health, long life, and wealth command.

Thro' the moss-agate's charm, the happy years
Ne'er see June's golden sunshine turn to tears.

JULY

Natal stone ....Turquoise.
Guardian angel ....Verchiel.
His talismanic gem ....Sapphire.
Special apostle ....Matthew.
His gem ....Topaz.
Zodiacal sign ....Leo.
Flower ....Water-lily.

The heav'n-blue turquoise should adorn
All those who in July are born;
For those they'll be exempt and free
From love's doubts and anxiety.

No other gem than turquoise on her breast
Can to the loving, doubting heart bring rest.

AUGUST

Natal stone ....Carnelian.
Guardian angel ....Hamatiel.
His talismanic gem ....Diamond.
Special apostle ....James, the son of Alpheus.
His gem ....Sardonyx.
Zodiacal sign ....Virgo.
Flower ....Poppy.

Wear a carnelian or for thee
No conjugal felicity;
The August-born without this stone,
'Tis said, must live unloved, alone.

She, loving once and always, wears, if wise,
Carnelian—and her home is paradise.

SEPTEMBER

Natal stone ....Chrysolite.
Guardian angel ....Tsuriel.
His talismanic gem ....Jacinth.
Special apostle ....Lebbeus Thaddeus.
His gem ....Chrysoprase.
Zodiacal sign ....Libra.
Flower ....Morning-glory.

A maid born when September leaves
Are rustling in the autumn breeze,
A chrysolite on brow should bind—
'Twill cure diseases of the mind.

If chrysolite upon her brow is laid,
Follies and dark delusions flee afraid.

OCTOBER

Natal stone ....Beryl.
Guardian angel ....Bariel.
His talismanic gem ....Agate.
Special apostle ....Simon. (Zelotes.)
His gem ....Jacinth.
Zodiacal sign ....Scorpio.
Flower ....Hops.

October's child is born for woe,
And life's vicissitudes must know;
But lay a beryl on her breast,
And Hope will lull those woes to rest.

When fair October to her brings the beryl,
No longer need she fear misfortune's peril.

NOVEMBER

Natal stone ....Topaz.
Guardian angel ....Adnachiel.
His talismanic gem ....Amethyst.
Special apostle ....Matthias.
His gem ....Amethyst.
Zodiacal sign ....Sagittarius.
Flower ....Chrysanthemum.

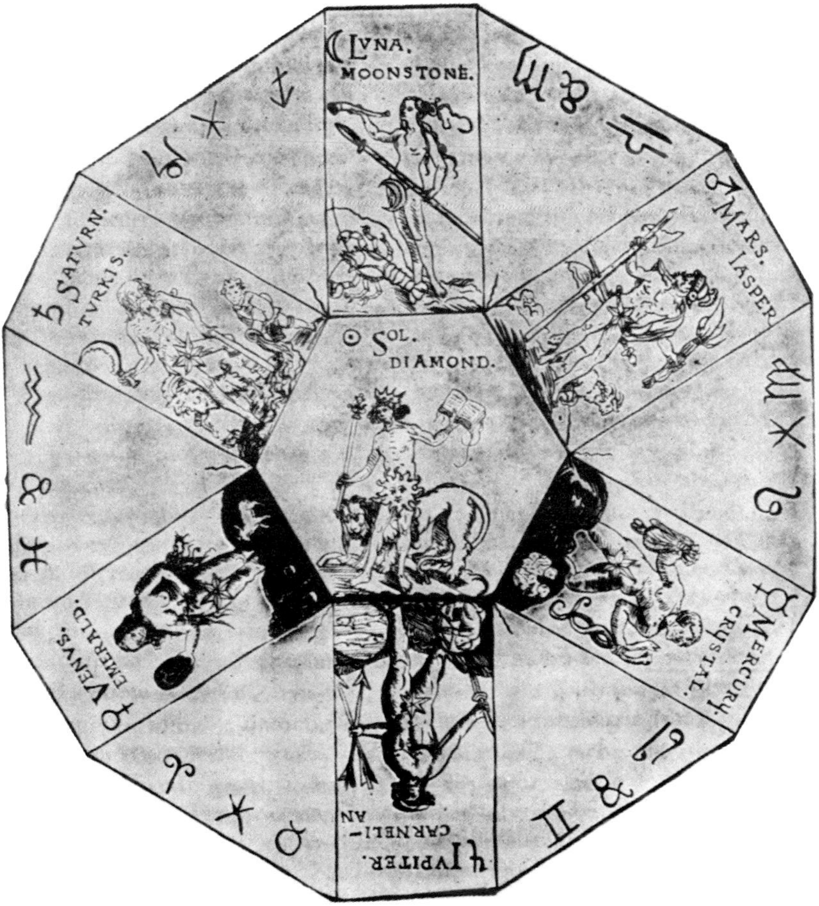

THE FIGURES OF THE PLANETS WITH THEIR SIGNIFICANT STONES.

Old print showing the Roman types of the days of the week and also the stones and zodiacal signs associated with each day. Here we have Diana, with the sign of Cancer and the moonstone, for Monday; Mars, with the sign Capricorn and the jasper, for Tuesday; Mercury, with Gemini and the rock-crystal, for Wednesday; Jupiter, with Sagittarius and Pisces and the carnelian, for Thursday; Venus, with Taurus and the emerald, for Friday; and Saturn, with Capricorn and Aquarius and the turquoise for Saturday.

Who first comes to this world below
With drear November's fog and snow
Should prize the topaz's amber hue—
Emblem of friends and lovers true.

Firm friendship is November's, and she bears
True love beneath the topaz that she wears.

DECEMBER

Natal stone	Ruby.
Guardian angel	Humiel.
His talismanic gem	Beryl.
Special apostle	Paul.
His gem	Sapphire.
Zodiacal sign	Capricornus.
Flower	Holly.

If cold December give you birth—
The month of snow and ice and mirth—
Place on your hand a ruby true;
Success will bless whate'er you do.

December gives her fortune, love and fame
If amulet of rubies bear her name.

A HINDU LIST OF GEMS OF THE MONTHS [11]

April	Diamond
May	Emerald
June	Pearl
July	Sapphire
August	Ruby
September	Zircon
October	Coral
November	Cat's-eye
December	Topaz
January	Serpent-stone
February	Chandrakanta
March	The gold Siva-linga

[11] Surindro Mohun Tagore, "Mani Málá," Pt. II, Calcutta, 1881, pp. 619, 621.

When the zodiacal signs were engraved on gems to give them special virtues and render them of greater efficacy for those born under a given sign, the Hebrew characters designating the sign (or at least the initial character) were often cut upon the gem. As the letters in which the earliest of our sacred writings were written, a peculiar sanctity was often ascribed to these Hebrew characters, which were perhaps the more highly valued that they were unknown to the owners of the gems, and hence possessed a certain air of mystery for them. The subjoined list of the signs with the Hebrew equivalents may be of interest on this account.

HEBREW NAMES OF THE SIGNS OF THE ZODIAC

Libra........................	מאזנים	Moznayim
Scorpio......................	עקרב	Åkrab
Sagittarius..................	קשת	Keshet
Capricornus..................	גדי	Ġedi
Aquarius.....................	דלי	Deli
Pisces.......................	דגים	Dagim
Aries........................	טלה	Taleh
Taurus.......................	שור	Ṡhor
Gemini.......................	תאומים	Te'omim
Cancer.......................	סרטן	Sartan
Leo..........................	אריה	Aryėh
Virgo........................	בתולה	Betulah

GEMS OF WEEK DAYS

Sunday: Topaz—diamond.

The bairn that is born
On Sonnan's sweet day
Is blithe and is bonnie,
Is happy and gay.

Sunday's talismanic gem: the pearl.

Monday: Pearl—crystal.

The bairn that is born
Of Monan's sweet race
Is lovely in feature
And fair in the face.

Monday's talismanic gem: the emerald.

Tuesday: Ruby—emerald.

If Tuisco assists
  And at birth keeps apace,
The bairn will be born
  With a soul full of grace.

Tuesday's talismanic gem: the topaz.

Wednesday: Amethyst—loadstone.

But if Woden be there,
  Many tears will he sow,
And the bairn will be born
  But for sadness and woe.

Wednesday's talismanic gem: the turquoise.

Thursday: Sapphire—carnelian.

Jove's presence at birth
  Means a long swath to mow,
For if born on Thor's day
  Thou hast far, far to go.

Thursday's talismanic gem: the sapphire.

Friday: Emerald—cat's-eye.

If Venus shall bless thee,
  Thou shalt bless many living;
For Friga's bairn truly
  Is loving and giving.

Friday's talismanic gem: the ruby.

Saturday: Turquoise—diamond.

Seater-daeg's bairn
  In sweat shall be striving,
For Saturn has doomed it
  To work for a living.

Saturday's talismanic gem: the amethyst.

No gems have afforded more interest to the Oriental peoples than those that are known as phenomenal gems; that is, such as exhibit a phenomenal quality, either as a moving line as in the chrysoberyl cat's-eye, or the quartz cat's-eye, or as a star, a class represented by the star-sapphire and the star-ruby, all these being considered to bring good fortune to the wearer. A splendid star-sapphire is in the hilt of the sword presented as an Easter gift to King Constantine of Greece, then Prince Constantine, by the Greeks of America, on Easter Day 1913.[12] This ornate and beautiful sword was made by Tiffany & Co. Then there is the alexandrite cat's-eye which, in addition to its chatoyant effect, changes from green to red, showing its natural color by day and glowing with a ruddy hue by artificial light. The cat's-eye effect here is caused by a twinning of the crystal; that is, when the gem is cut, with a dome, across the twinning line, this shows itself as a smooth band of white light, with a translucent or transparent space at one side, the line varying in sharpness and in breadth as the illumination becomes more intense. If the light is very bright, the line is no wider than the thinnest possible silver or platinum wire.

The quartz cat's-eye, less distinct than the chrysoberyl cat's-eye, is also found in the East, and possesses the property that when cut straight across, an apparent striation in the stone produces the cat's-eye effect, but the material is not so rich or brilliant nor is the gem as beautiful as is the true cat's-eye. The alexandrite variety of chrysoberyl is colored by chromium and is dichroitic, appearing green when viewed in one direction and red in another; in artificial light, however, the green color is lost and the red alone becomes apparent.

The moonstone, with its moonlike, silvery-white light, changes on the surface as the light varies. This is due to a chatoyancy produced by a reflection caused by certain cleavage planes present in feldspar of the variety to which the moonstone belongs.

---

[12] The star-sapphire has already been described on pp. 106, 107.

PHENOMENAL GEMS FOR THE DAYS OF THE WEEK

Sunday	Sunstone
Monday	Moonstone
Tuesday	Star sapphire
Wednesday	Star ruby
Thursday	Cat's-eye
Friday	Alexandrite
Saturday	Labradorite

Fashion in some parts of the Orient dictates the use of special colors for raiment and jewels to be worn on the different days of the week. In Siam deep red silks and rubies are appropriate for Sunday wear; white fabrics and moonstones are prescribed for Monday; light red garments and coral ornaments are favored for Tuesday; striped stuffs and jewels set with the cat's-eye are considered the proper wear for Wednesday; green materials and emeralds are decreed for Thursday; silver-blue robes and ornaments set with diamonds are chosen for Friday, and on Saturday those who obey the dictates of fashion are clad in dark blue garments and wear sapphires of a similar hue.

Our age is not satisfied with the marvellous progress of science, which has rendered possible the realization of many of the old magicians' dreams. In spite of this there seems to be a growing tendency to revive many of the old beliefs which appeared to have been definitely discarded; therefore we need not be surprised that the nineteenth century offers us a work on the magic art, written precisely in the spirit that animated an Agrippa or a Porta in the fifteenth and sixteenth centuries.[13] This work gives elaborate directions as to the manner in which the "Magus" should proceed to perform his magic rites.

[13] Eliphas Lévi, "Rituel de la haute magie," Paris, 1861.

Each day has its special and peculiar ritual. Sunday is the day for the "Works of Light," and on this day a purple robe should be worn and a tiara and bracelets of gold; the ring placed on the finger of the operator should be of gold and set with a chrysolite or a ruby. A white robe with silver stripes is to be worn on Monday, the day of the "Works of Divination and Mystery," and the high-priest of the mysteries wears over his robe a triple necklace of pearls, "crystals," and selenites; the tiara should be covered with yellow silk, and bear in silver characters the Hebrew monogram of Gabriel, as given by Cornelius Agrippa in his "Occult Philosophy." Tuesday is assigned to the "Works of Wrath," and on this day the robe must be red, the color of fire and blood, with a belt and bracelets of steel; the tiara should have a circlet of iron, and a sword or a stylus is to be used in place of a wand; the ring is set with an amethyst. The day for the "Works of Science" is Wednesday, when a green robe is worn and a necklace of hollow glass beads, filled with quicksilver; the ring is adorned with an agate. On Thursday, appointed for the "Works of Religion or Politics," a scarlet robe is worn; upon the forehead of the operator is bound a plate of tin, engraved with the symbol of the planet Jupiter and various mystic characters; the ring bears either an emerald or a sapphire. Friday, the day of Venus, is naturally dedicated to the "Works of Love," and the celebrant wears a sky-blue robe; his ring shows a turquoise, and his tiara is set with lapis-lazuli and beryl. The "Works of Mourning" belong to Saturday, when a black or a brown robe is worn, embroidered in orange-colored silk with mystic characters; from the neck of the operator hangs a leaden medal, bearing the symbol of the planet Saturn, and on his finger is a ring set with an onyx, upon which a double-faced Janus has been engraved while Saturn was in the ascendant.

GEMS OF THE HOURS

Hours of the Day

7	Chrysolite	1	Jacinth
8	Amethyst	2	Emerald
9	Kunzite	3	Beryl
10	Sapphire	4	Topaz
11	Garnet	5	Ruby
12	Diamond	6	Opal

Hours of the Night

7	Sardonyx	1	Morion
8	Chalcedony	2	Hematite
9	Jade	3	Malachite
10	Jasper	4	Lapis-lazuli
11	Loadstone	5	Turquoise
12	Onyx	6	Tourmaline

WEDDING ANNIVERSARIES

1	Paper	19	Hyacinth
2	Calico	20	China
3	Linen	23	Sapphire
4	Silk	25	Silver
5	Wood	26	Star sapphire, blue *
6	Candy	30	Pearl
7	Floral	35	Coral
8	Leather	39	Cat's-eye *
9	Straw	40	Ruby
10	Tin	45	Alexandrite
12	Agate	50	Gold
13	Moonstone *	52	Star ruby *
14	Moss agate	55	Emerald
15	Rock-crystal, glass	60	Diamond, yellow
16	Topaz	65	Star sapphire, gray *
17	Amethyst	67	Star sapphire, purple
18	Garnet	75	Diamond

* For this number, and for the succeeding multiples of thirteen, the gem is believed to counteract the malign influence of the number.

IV

Planetary and Astral Influences of Precious Stones

THE talismanic influence of the stones associated with the planets and also with the signs of the zodiac is closely connected with the early ideas regarding the formation of precious stones. In an old work on the occult properties of gems we read:

> The nature of the magnet is in the iron, and the nature of the iron is in the magnet, and the nature of both polar stars is in both iron and magnet, and hence the nature of the iron and the magnet is also in both polar stars, and since they are Martian, that is to say, their region belongs to Mars, so do both iron and magnet belong to Mars.

The author then proceeds to describe an analogous relation between a man and any natural object or product to which his imagination draws him, and shows that, if this object be one that stands in a sympathetic relation with the star beneath which the man was born, the man, the star, and the object will constitute a triplicity of great utility. As an explanation of the peculiarly intimate relation between stars and precious stones we read, on page 12:

> Metals and precious stones usually lie with their first seeds deep down in the earth and require continuous moisture and a mild heat. This they obtain through a reflection of the sun and the other stars in the manifold movement of the heavens. . . . Therefore, also, the metals and precious stones are nearest related to the planets

and the stars, since these influence them most potently and produce their peculiar qualities, for they are enduring and unchangeable and show therein their concordance [with the stars and the planets].[1]

Hence it is that the influence over human fortunes ascribed by astrology to the heavenly bodies is conceived to be strengthened by wearing the gem appropriate to certain planets or signs, for a subtle emanation has passed into the stone and radiates from it. A combination of several different stones, each partaking of this special quality, was believed to have an influence similar to that exercised by several planets in conjunction,—that is, grouped in the same "house" or division of the heavens.

The same is true of the stones dedicated to the guardian angels; the color and appearance of the stone was not merely emblematic of the angel, but, by its sympathetic quality, it was supposed to attract his influence and to provide a medium for the transmission of his beneficent force to the wearer. The whole theory, whether consciously or unconsciously, rested on the idea of harmony, of the accord of certain ethereal vibrations, either those of the visible light of the stars and planets or the purely psychic emanations from the spiritual "powers and principalities."

The wearing of the appropriate zodiacal gem was always believed to strengthen the influence of the zodiacal sign upon those born under it, and to afford a sympathetic medium for the transmission of the stellar influences. The gem was thus something more than a mere symbol of the sign. The same was true of the stone of the saint who ruled the month and that of the holy guar-

[1] Wilhelmus Eo, "Coronæ Gemma Nobilissima," Newheusern, 1621, pp. 38–9.

dian angel set over those born in the month. In each and every case the material form and color of the stone was believed to attract the favor and grace of the saint or angel, who would see in the selection of the appropriate gem an act of respect and veneration on the part of the wearer.

The old writers are never tired of insisting upon the idea that, while the image graven upon a stone was in itself dead and inactive, the influence of the stars during whose ascendancy the work had been executed communicated to the inert material talismanic qualities and virtues which it before lacked. In these instances the images could be regarded as outward and visible signs of the planetary or zodiacal influence. Even in the case of the bezoar stone, a generally recognized antidote for all sorts of poisons, it was held that the scorpion's bite could be most effectually healed by a bezoar upon which this creature's figure had been cut during the time when the constellation Scorpio was in the ascendancy.[2]

In the production of engraved stones to serve as amulets, the influence of the respective planet was made to enter the stone by casting upon the latter, during the process of engraving, reflections from a mirror which had been exposed to the planet's rays. In addition to this, the work was executed while the planet was in the ascendant, and the design was emblematic of it. With these combined influences the gem was believed to be thoroughly impregnated with the planetary virtue.[3]

An old writer finds in the hardness of precious stones a reason for their retaining longer the celestial virtues they receive. After they have been extracted these vir-

---

[2] Gaffarelli, "Curiositates inauditæ," Hamburgi, 1706, pp. 146, 147.

[3] Schindler, "Der Aberglaube des Mittelalters," Breslau, 1858, p. 131.

tues persist in them and they keep "the traces and gifts of mundane life which they possessed while clinging to the earth.[4] These "gifts of mundane life" signify the stored-up energy derived from the stars and planets, which penetrates the matter of the stone, and each stone is peculiarly sensitive to the emanations from a certain planet, star, or group of stars.

A fine carnelian gem engraved with a design consisting of a star surrounded by the images of a ram, a bull, and a lion, is described by M. Mairan.[5] He sees in the star the emblem of the splendid comet which appeared shortly after the assassination of Cæsar, and which, according to Suetonius, was believed to be the soul of Cæsar newly received into the sky; the ram, bull, and lion are the symbols of the zodiacal signs Aries, Taurus, and Leo, the first-named sign referring perhaps to the death of Cæsar on the Ides, or fifteenth of March; while the other two signs may allude to the position of the comet at different dates.

In the Cabinet du Roi, in Paris, there was an engraved carnelian, the design showing Jupiter enthroned, with thunderbolt and sceptre, and Mars and Mercury standing on either side of the central figure. Separated from the gods of the upper air by a bow, probably representing the arch of the sky, appears the bust of Neptune, emerging from the sea. The border of the design is formed by the twelve signs of the zodiac, Virgo being of an unusual type,—the virgin and a unicorn,—said to have been used only during the reign of Domitian (81–96 A.D.).[6]

---

[4] Reichelti, "De amuletis," Argentorati, 1676, p. 45; citing Ficini, "De vita coelit.," cap. 13.

[5] Mairan, "Lettres au R. P. Parrenin," Paris, 1770, pp. 275 sqq.

[6] Mairan, l.c., pp. 199, 211.

Some choice examples of astrological gems may be seen in the Metropolitan Museum of Art, New York; among these is a green jasper bearing symbols of Luna, Capricorn, and Taurus. This gem is from the collection of the late Rev. C. W. King, which has been acquired for the Museum, and is described as figuring the horoscope of the owner. In the same collection is a banded agate engraved with Sagittarius as a centaur, surrounded by the stars of this constellation in their proper order. King states that this was the earliest horoscopical gem known to him. Still another gem of this collection is a sard bearing the symbol of Aries carrying a long caduceus; this type appears on the coins of Antioch, because that city was founded in the month over which the sign Aries presides.[7]

The Austrian Imperial Collection in Vienna contains the celebrated Gemma Augustea, sometimes called the Apotheosis of Augustus. This commemorates the Pannonian triumph of Tiberius, 13 A.D., and above the figure of Augustus appears the sign of Capricornus, the constellation of his nativity; beneath the figure of Tiberius is engraved the sign of Scorpio, under which that emperor was born. This celebrated cameo, the work of the famous gem-engraver Dioskorides, is mentioned in an inventory of the treasury of St. Sernin, in Toulouse, dated 1246. It is said to have been offered by Francis I of France to Pope Clement VII, on the occasion of their meeting in Marseilles in 1535; however, as the gem only reached Marseilles two days after the pope's departure, Francis decided to retain possession of it. The

[7] "Collection of Engraved Gems," Metropolitan Museum of Art, Handbook No. 9, pp. 53, 54.

THE ZODIACAL STONES WITH THEIR SIGNS.

Old print illustrating the influence believed to be exerted on the different parts of the body by the respective zodiacal signs, and through their power by the stones associated with them. This belief often determined the administration of special precious-stone remedies by physicians of the seventeenth and earlier centuries.

royal treasure at Fontainebleau was plundered in 1590, and the stone was offered for sale, and was purchased, in 1619, by Emperor Rudolph II, for the sum of 12,000 ducats.

A ruby called sandastros is described by Pliny as containing stellated bodies which he compares to the Hyades; hence, says he, they are the objects of great devotion with the Chaldæi or Assyrian Magi. According to Morales (De las piedras preciosas), the ruby and the diamond were both under the influence of the sign of Taurus; the same writer informs us that the Hyades and the sun were supposed to have a potent effect upon the ruby or carbuncle. In ancient Babylonia the sign of Taurus was regarded as the most important, and Winckler believes that the presence in this sign of the five stars of the Hyades and the seven of the Pleiades was brought into connection with the twelve-fold division of the zodiac. The Hyades signified the five signs visible in Babylonia at the summer solstice, while the Pleiades typified the seven invisible signs. It seems probable that the Pleiades were associated with the diamond, although Morales, who was very familiar with the Moorish astrology current among the Spaniards of his time, attributed the crystal to this group. His attribution proves at least that the stone of the Pleiades was a colorless one.

In Sanskrit the diamond is called *vajra*, "thunderbolt," and also *indrâjudha*, "Indra's weapon"; another name is *açira*, "fire," or "the Sun."[8] All these designations are probably suggested by the brilliant flashes of

[8] Garbe, "Die indische Mineralien," Naharari's Râjanighantu, Varga XIII, Leipzig, 1882, p. 80.

light emitted by this stone. It is not easy to determine the reason that induced the Hindus to dedicate the diamond to the planet Venus rather than to the Sun or to the Moon. However, as the most brilliant of the planets, Venus was not unworthy of the honor, and if we substitute the Goddess of Love for her planet, it seems quite appropriate that she should be adorned with the most brilliant of precious stones. Certainly these sparkling gems are often enough offered at the shrine of Venus in our own day, and they often serve to win the good graces of the divinity to whom they are presented.

The Sanskrit name for the sapphire, *nîla,* signifies "blue," so that, as the topaz is the "yellow stone" *par excellence,* the sapphire is the blue stone (*nilaçman*). In both cases the name indicates a variety of corundum, distinguished merely by the coloring matter. As a talisman the Hindus believed that the sapphire rendered the planet Saturn favorable to the wearer, an important consideration from the astrological point of view, for Saturn's influence was generally supposed to be unfavorable. The Hindus distinguished four classes of sapphires, corresponding to the four castes: Brahmins, Kshatriyas, Vaisyas, and Sudras. The respective sapphires were light blue, reddish blue, yellowish blue, and dark blue. The same distinction is made in the case of the diamond, and a like rule applies to both stones, namely, that only the appropriate stone should be worn by the members of each caste, in order to profit by the virtues inherent in the sapphire or diamond.[9]

One of the Sanskrit appellations of the hyacinth (zircon) is *râhuratna,*—that is, the jewel dedicated to the mysterious "dragon," that was supposed to be the

[9] Garbe, "Die indische Mineralien," Naharari's Râjanighantu, Varga XIII, Leipzig, 1882, p. 83.

cause of the periodic eclipses of the Sun and Moon.[10] As the stone was sacred to this malevolent influence, we need not be surprised that it was believed to avert misfortune, for nothing was so effective against the lesser spirits of evil as an evil genius of great power.

According to the Hindu mystics it was very lucky to have a turquoise at hand at the time of the new moon, for whoever, after first looking at the moon on the *pratipada* (the first day after new-moon), should cast his eyes upon a turquoise, was destined to enjoy immeasurable wealth.[11]

ZODIACAL GEMS

Aquarius.
January 21 to February 21.
The Garnet.

If you would cherish friendship true,
In Aquarius well you'll do
To wear this gem of warmest hue—
The garnet.

Pisces.
February 21 to March 21.
The Amethyst.

From passion and from care kept free
Shall Pisces' children ever be
Who wear so all the world may see
The amethyst.

Aries.
March 21 to April 20.
The Bloodstone.

Who on this world of ours his eyes
In Aries opens shall be wise
If always on his hand there lies
A bloodstone.

---

[10] Garbe, "Die indische Mineralien," Naharari's Râjanighantu, Varga XIII, Leipzig, 1882, p. 84.

[11] Surindro Mohun Tagore, "Mani Málá," Pt. II, Calcutta, 1881, p. 883.

Taurus.

April 20 to May 21.

The Sapphire.

If on your hand this stone you bind,
You in Taurus born will find
'Twill cure diseases of the mind,
The sapphire.

Gemini.

May 21 to June 21.

The Agate.

Gemini's children health and wealth command,
And all the ills of age withstand,
Who wear their rings on either hand
Of agate.

Cancer.

June 21 to July 22.

The Emerald.

If born in Cancer's sign, they say,
Your life will joyful be alway,
If you take with you on your way
An emerald.

Leo.

July 22 to August 22.

The Onyx.

When youth to manhood shall have grown,
Under Leo lorn and lone
'Twill have lived but for this stone,
The onyx.

Virgo.

August 22 to September 22.

Carnelian.

Success will bless whate'er you do,
Through Virgo's sign, if only you
Place on your hand her own gem true,
Carnelian.

Libra.

September 22 to October 23.

The Chrysolite.

Through Libra's sign it is quite well
To free yourself from evil spell,
For in her gem surcease doth dwell,
The chrysolite.

1. A necklace of banded and variegated agates, onyx, carnelians and sards. First Century A.D.
2. Beads of carnelian artificially marked for "good luck." The marking is produced by an application of potash and soda. Ancient Persian.

Scorpio.
October 23 to November 21.
The Beryl.

Through Scorpio this gem so fair
Is that which every one should wear,
Or tears of sad repentance bear,—
The beryl.

Sagittarius.
November 21 to December 21.
The Topaz.

Who first comes to this world below
Under Sagittarius should know
That their true gem should ever show
A topaz.

Capricorn.
December 21 to January 21.
The Ruby.

Those who live in Capricorn
No trouble shall their brows adorn
If they this glowing gem have worn,
The ruby.

An old Spanish list of the gems of the zodiacal signs differs from those given above, and probably represents Arab tradition: [12]

Aries—Crystal	Libra—Jasper
Taurus—Ruby and diamond	Scorpio—Garnet
Gemini—Sapphire	Sagittarius—Emerald
Cancer—Agate and beryl	Capricorn—Chalcedony
Leo—Topaz	Aquarius—Amethyst
Virgo—Magnet	Pisces—

Of planetary stones [13] there is assigned to the sun the jacinth and the chrysolite, when this latter name

[12] Morales, "De las virtudes y propiedades marvillosas de las piedras preciosas," Valladolid, 1604, fols. 15a, 15b.

[13] Rantzau, "Tractatus de genethliacorum thematum judiciis," Francofurti, 1633, pp. 46–55.

was applied to the yellow Brazilian chrysoberyl, while the moon controls the beryl, the rock-crystal and also the pearl. To the share of Venus fall the sapphire and carbuncle as well as coral and pearl; usually the emerald is the stone of Venus. Mars lays claim to the diamond, jacinth, and ruby, the last-named stone according with the ruddy hue of our neighbor planet. Under the control of Jupiter are placed the emerald, sapphire, amethyst, and turquoise, so that this planet has the richest assortment of gems; it will be remarked that the celestial sapphire unites the influence of Venus and Jupiter, the two especially propitious planets. Lastly, far-away Saturn must be content with all dark, black, and brittle stones; there was, indeed, little inducement to wear a Saturnian stone, for the influence of this cold and distant planet was always regarded as baleful.

The planetary controls of precious stones as given in the Lapidario of Alfonso X, according to "Chaldaic" tradition, show that the same stone was influenced in many or most cases by more than one of the "seven planets" (including the Sun and Moon). Thus the diamond, belonging to the first degree of the sign Taurus, was dominated by both Saturn and the Sun; the emerald was controlled by Jupiter, and also by Mercury and by Venus. The red jargoon was influenced by Mars, the yellow variety by Jupiter and the white jargoon by Venus. The carnelian received virtue from the Sun and from Venus. The ruby, although more especially a sunstone, came as well under the influence of the Planet of Love. Coral belonged both to Venus and to the moon, while lapis-lazuli and chalcedony only owed allegiance to Venus; this planet also lent virtue to the beryl.[14]

---

[14] Lapidario del Rey D. Alfonso X; codice original, Madrid, 1881, fols. 101–109.

Among the Mohammedans, six of the seven heavens were supposed to be made of precious substances: the first was of emerald; the second, of white silver; the third, of large white pearls; the fourth, of ruby; the fifth, of red gold; and the sixth, of jacinth. The seventh and highest heaven, however, was of shining light.[15] Here we have the three precious colored stones, emerald, ruby, and sapphire (jacinth), to which is added the pearl.

The scarcity of the diamond in early times, and its comparative lack of brilliancy before the invention of rose and brilliant cutting, account for the absence of this king of gems.

Rabelais,[16] describing the temple of the oracle of the "Dive Bouteille," says that of its seven columns the first was of sapphire; the second, of jacinth; the third, of "dyamant"; the fourth, of the "male" balas-ruby; the fifth, of emerald, "more brilliant and glistening than were those which were set in place of eyes in the marble lion stretched before the tomb of King Hermias"; the sixth column was of agate, and the seventh of transparent selenite, " with a splendor like that of Hymettian honey, and within appeared the moon in form and motion such as she is in the heavens, full and new, waxing and waning." We are then told that these stones were attributed to the seven planets by the Chaldæans, as follows:

Sapphire .... Saturn
Jacinth .... Jupiter
Diamond .... Sun
Ruby .... Mars

---

[15] Lane, "Arabian Society in the Middle Ages," ed. by Stanley Lane-Poole, London, 1883, p. 98.

[16] Pantagruel, liv. v, chap. xlii, Paris, 1833, p. 341.

Emerald	Venus
Agate	Mercury
Selenite	Moon

Some of these attributions differ from those usually made and may represent another tradition.

PLANETARY INFLUENCES OF STONES [17]

Jasper	Venus and Mercury.
Sapphire	Jupiter and Mercury.
Emerald	Venus and Mercury.
Chalcedony	Jupiter, Mercury, and Saturn.
Sardonyx	Saturn and Mars.
Chrysolite	Mercury and Venus.
Beryl	Venus and Mars.
Topaz	Saturn and Mars.
Chrysoprase	Mercury and Venus.
Jacinth	Mars and Jupiter.
Amethyst	Mars and Jupiter.
Pearl	Venus and Mercury.
Carbuncle	Mars and Venus.
Diamond	Jupiter.
Agate	Venus and Mars.
Alectoria	Sun.
Turquoise	Venus and Mercury.
Chelidon	Jupiter.
Aetites	Sun.
Dionesia	Saturn.
Hematite	Mercury.
Lapis-lazuli	Venus.
Armena	Mercury and Venus.
Garnet	Sun.
Amber	Sun.
Jet	Saturn.
Lyncurius	Sun.
Crystal	Moon and Mars.
Bezoar	Jupiter.
Armenia.	Jupiter.

[17] Morales, "De las Piedras Preciosas," Valladolid, 1604.

Selenite	Moon.
Magnet	Mars.
Judaica, Hegolite or Cogolite	Mercury.
Iris	Jupiter.
Halcyon	Saturn and Mars.
Asbestus	Saturn.
Sarcophagus	Moon.
Arabian, white	Moon.
Arabian, green	Jupiter
Hyena	Sun.
Androdamas	Moon.
Pyrites:	
Copper-colored	Sun, Venus.
Gold-colored	Sun.
Silver-colored	Moon.
Tin-colored	Moon, Saturn.
Ash-colored	Jupiter.
Calatia	Moon.
Stalactite	Venus.
Thenarcus	Sun.
Carnelian	Jupiter, Mars, Venus.
Opal	Sun, Mercury.

Fixed stars associated with precious stones:[18]

Diamond. Caput Algol 18° of Taurus.
Crystal. The Pleiades 24° of Taurus.
Ruby, carbuncle. Aldebaran 3° of Gemini; also the Hyades.
Sapphire. The Goat 15° of Gemini.
Beryl. Sirius 10° of Cancer.
Garnet. Heart of Lion 23° of Leo.
Magnet. Tail of the Great Bear 8° of Scorpio; also the Pole Star.
Topaz. Right and left wing of Raven 8° of Libra.
Emerald and Jasper. Spica Virginis 17° of Libra.
Amethyst. Scorpion 3° of Sagittarius.
Chrysolite. Tortoise 8° of Capricorn.

---

[18] Morales, "De las piedras preciosas," Valladolid, 1604, pp. 16a-16b.

Chalcedony. Tail of Capricorn 15° of Aquarius.
Jacinth. Shoulder of Equis Major 18° of Pisces.
Pearl. Umbilicus Andromedæ 20° of Aries.
Sardonyx. Same as Topaz.

Images and virtues of the constellations as engraved on gems: [19]

URSA MAJOR, URSA MINOR, AND DRACO. Both bears are represented in the folds of a serpent, the Great Bear in the upper and the Lesser Bear in the lower folds. In almost all the signs. Nature: Ursa Major, Mars and Venus. Ursa Minor; Saturn. Draco: Saturn and Mars. Renders the wearer wise, cautious, versatile, and powerful.

The boundary lines of the various signs are carried up to the pole, and any constellation that is within these lines is considered to belong to the respective sign; thus, every constellation belongs to one or more signs.

CORONA BOREALIS. A royal crown, with many stars; sometimes the crowned head of a king. Sign: Sagittarius. Nature: Venus and Mercury. Engraved on the stone of one who is fitted for honors and knowledge, it gives him great favor with kings.

HERCULES. A man with knees bent, holding a club in his hand and killing a lion; sometimes a man with a lion's skin in his hand or on his shoulder and holding a club. Sign: Scorpio. Nature: Venus and Mercury. Engraved on a stone that brings victory, like the agate, it renders the wearer victorious in all conflicts in the field.

CYGNUS. A swan with outstretched wings and curved neck. In the North. Nature: Venus and Mercury. Renders the wearer popular, increases knowledge, and augments wealth. Cures gout, paralysis, and fever.

---

[19] Camilli Leonardi, "Speculum Lapidum," Venetia, 1502, f. liv–lvi.

Cepheus. A man girt with a sword and holding his hands and arms extended. Sign: Aries. Nature: Saturn and Jupiter. Causes pleasant visions if placed beneath the head of a sleeping person.

Cassiopeia. A woman seated in a chair and with hands extended in the form of a cross; sometimes with a triangle on her head. Sign: Taurus. Nature: Saturn and Venus. Restores the sickly, worn body to health, gives quiet and calm after labor and procures pleasant and tranquil sleep.

Andromeda. A young girl with dishevelled hair, and hands hanging down. Sign: Taurus. Nature: Venus. Reconciles husband and wife, strengthens love, and protects the human body from many diseases.

Perseus. A man holding a sword in his right hand and the Gorgon's head in his left. Sign: Taurus. Nature: Saturn and Venus. Guards the wearer from misfortune and protects, not only the wearer but the place where it may be, from lightning and tempest. Dissolves enchantments.

Serpens. A man in the folds of a serpent and holding its head in his right hand and its tail in his left. Sign: Taurus. Nature: Saturn and Venus. Antidote to poisons and to the bites of venomous creatures.

Aquila. A flying eagle with an arrow beneath his feet. Sign: Cancer. Nature: Jupiter and Mercury; the arrow, however, is of Mars and Venus. Preserves former honors, adds new ones, and helps to victory.

Pisces or Delphinus. Figured in relief (?) Sign: Aquarius. Nature: Saturn and Mars. If this engraved gem be attached to nets it causes them to be filled with fish, and it renders the wearer fortunate in fishing.

Pegasus. Some represent the half of a winged horse; others the whole figure and without a bridle. Sign: Aries. Nature: Mars and Jupiter. Gives victory in the field, and makes the wearer swift, cautious, and bold.

CETUS. Figure of a large fish with curved tail and capacious gullet. Sign: Taurus. Nature: Saturn. Renders the wearer fortunate on the sea and makes him prudent and agreeable. It also restores lost articles.

ORION. With or without armor, man holding a sword or a scythe in his hand. Sign: Gemini. Nature: Jupiter, Saturn, and Mars. Gives the wearer victory over his enemies.

NAVIS. A ship with prow curved back and spread sails; sometimes with and sometimes without oars. Sign: Leo. Nature: Saturn and Jupiter. Renders the wearer fortunate in his undertakings; he runs no risk on sea or water, neither can he be injured by water.

CANIS MAJOR. Figure of a dog for coursing hares, with a curved tail. Sign: Cancer. Nature: Venus. Cures lunacy, insanity, and demoniacal possession.

LEPUS. Figure of a hare with ears pricked up and the feet represented as though in swift motion. Sign: Gemini. Nature: Saturn and Mercury. Cures frenzy and protects from the wiles of demons. The wearer cannot be hurt by a malignant spirit.

CENTAUR. Half-figure of a bull, bearing a man on whose left shoulder rests a lance, from which depends a hare. In his right hand the man holds a small, supine animal with a vessel attached to it. Sign: Libra. Nature: Jupiter and Mars. Gives constancy and perpetual health.

CANIS MINOR. Figure of a dog, sitting. Sign: Cancer. Nature: Jupiter. Guards from dropsy, pestilence, and the bites of dogs.

SACRARIUS TURUBULUS (ARA). An altar with burning incense. Sign: Sagittarius. Nature: Venus and Mercury. Gives the wearer power to recognize spirits, to converse with them, and to command them; also confers chastity.

HYDRA. A serpent, having an urn at its head and a raven at its tail. Sign: Cancer. Nature: Saturn and Venus. Gives riches and all good gifts to the wearer and makes him cautious and prudent.

CORONA AUSTRALIS. An imperial crown. Sign: Libra. Nature: Saturn and Mars. Augments wealth and makes the wearer gay and happy.

AURIGA. A man in a chariot, bearing a goat on his left shoulder. Sign: Gemini. Nature: Mercury. Makes the wearer successful in hunting.

VEXILLUM. A flag flying from the extremity of a lance Sign: Scorpion. Gives skill in war and confers victory in the field.

FIGURES OF THE PLANETS

SATURN. An old man holding a curved scythe in his hand and with a not very heavy beard. Engraved on a stone of the nature of Saturn, it renders the wearer powerful and augments his power continually.

JUPITER. A seated figure, sometimes in a chariot, holding a staff in one hand and a spear in the other. It renders the wearer fortunate, especially if engraved on a Kabratis stone, and he easily gains what he wishes, especially from priests. He will be raised to honors and dignities.

MARS. Represented sometimes with a banner and sometimes with a lance or other weapon. He is, indeed, always armed and at times mounted on a horse. Gives victory, boldness in war, and success in everything, especially if engraved on an appropriate stone.

SUN. Sometimes as the solar disk with rays, sometimes as a man in a chariot, and this occasionally is surrounded by the signs of the zodiac. Renders the wearer powerful and a victor; this gem is prized by hunters.

VENUS Many forms, among them that of a woman with a voluminous dress and a stole, holding a laurel in her hand. Gives skill in handling affairs and usually brings them to a successful issue; removes the fear of drowning.

MERCURY. Figure of a slender man, usually with a beautiful beard, but sometimes without. He has winged feet and holds the caduceus. Increases knowledge and confers eloquence. It aids merchants, enabling them to acquire wealth.

MOON. Various forms. Sometimes as a crescent, sometimes as a young woman in a chariot and holding a quiver, and at others as a woman with a quiver and following the chase with dogs. Aids the fortunes of those who are sent on an embassy, and enables them to acquire wealth and honor thereby. Is said to confer speed and facility in undertakings and a happy issue.[20]

When Hudibras attacked and overcame the sorcerer Sidrophal, he rifled the latter's pockets of all his mystic treasures. Among these were

> Several constellation stones,
> Engraved in planetary hours,
> That over mortals had strange powers,
> To make them thrive in law or trade,
> And stab or poison to evade,
> In wit and wisdom to improve,
> And be victorious in love.[21]

These manifold influences exerted by the stars and planets through the medium of the gems, not only concerned those actually present in a material form, but also those that were seen in dreams, and interpretations of such dreams are given by old writers.

Many Oneirocritica, or "dream-books," were written or compiled in the early centuries of our era, one of the most noted being the work of Artemidorus, who flourished in the second century A.D. Every object seen in a dream was given a special meaning, and it is interesting to note that Artemidorus believed dreams of rings or other ornaments, as well as of precious stones, to be of favorable significance only for women. Such dreams indicated marriage for unmarried women, and the birth

[20] Camilli Leonardi, "Speculum Lapidum," Venetia, 1502, f. liii.

[21] Butler, "Hudibras," Part II, Canto III, 11, 1096–1103.

of children for those already married. If a woman was both wife and mother when she saw sparkling jewels in her dream, then the vision portended the acquisition of great wealth. Artemidorus here sagely remarks that women are by nature devoted to riches and passionately fond of ornaments. For men, on the other hand, to dream of jewels was an ill omen; probably because it foreshadowed the necessity of buying them for a good friend or a faithful wife.[22]

Another of these dream-books, probably composed in the eighth century A.D., appears under the name of Achametis and is of Arabic origin. Many of the interpretations in this book are referred to a Hindu source, and among these are visions of crowns that appear to kings. Such a dream, in itself, usually portended increased power and success for the sovereign, but this depended upon the color and character of the jewels which adorned the crown. For example, we read that if the gems were red and of the kind known as lychnites (carbuncles or rubies), the dream indicated that the king would have great joy and good fortune and would be more feared by his enemies than before; but if he saw blue gems in the crown, it was a bad omen, foreshadowing the loss of part of his kingdom. If the stones were of a light green hue (the color of the leek), the king would gain a great name in the world, both by his good faith and by the greatness of his kingdom; for, the writer adds, "this color in precious stones is universally accepted as signifying good-faith and religious devotion to God."[23]

---

[22] Artemidori Daldiani et Achametis Sereimi Oneirocritica. ed. Regaltius, Lutetiæ, 1603, pp. 86, 87.

[23] Ibid., p. 228.

There is signified by dreaming of

Agates	A journey.
Amber	A voyage.
Amethysts	Freedom from harm.
Aquamarines	New friends.
Beryls	Happiness in store.
Bloodstones	Distressing news.
Carbuncles	Acquirement of wisdom.
Carnelians	Impending misfortune.
Cat's-eyes	Treachery.
Chalcedony	Friends rejoined.
Chrysoberyls	A time of need.
Chrysolites	Necessary caution.
Coral	Recovery from illness.
Crystal	Freedom from enemies.
Diamonds	Victory over enemies.
Emeralds	Much to look forward to.
Garnets	The solution of a mystery.
Heliotropes	Long life.
Hyacinths	A heavy storm.
Jacinths	Success.
Jasper	Love returned.
Jet	Sorrow.
Lapis-lazuli	Faithful love.
Moonstones	Impending danger.
Moss-agates	An unsuccessful journey.
Onyx	A happy marriage.
Opals	Great possessions.
Pearls	Faithful friends.
Porphyry	Death.
Rubies	Unexpected guests.
Sapphires	Escape from danger.
Sardonyx	Love of friends.
Topaz	No harm shall befall.
Tourmalines	An accident.
Turquoises	Prosperity.

If precious stones be so combined in a ring, or other jewel that the initial letters of their names spell words

STATUETTE KNOWN AS THAT OF SAINTE FOY, IN THE ABBEY-CHURCH AT CONQUES, DEPT. AVEYRON, FRANCE.

It is studded with precious and semi-precious stones and engraved gems, dating from various epochs, the pious offerings of those whose prayers have been answered. The figure is 85 cm. (33½ inches) high and is of gold in a core of wood. Probably of the tenth century. Two of the four crystal balls adorning the seat are said to replace golden doves. Rock-crystal was especially dedicated to the moon.

significant of a tender sentiment or implying good fortune, or else the name of someone dear to the giver of the jewel, this is also supposed to strengthen their astral or planetary influence and to render them more potent charms. In the following examples the gems in the first column are the more expensive, those in the second column being comparatively inexpensive ones.

ACROSTICS FORMED WITH STONES

In France and England, during the 18th century, rings, bracelets, brooches, etc., were often set with gems the first letters of which, combined, formed a motto or expressed a sentiment. The following is a list of those that may be used in this way. The choice of stones afforded here brings these pretty devices within the reach of all.

FAITH

Fire-opal.	Feldspar.
Alexandrite.	Amethyst.
Iolite.	Idocrase.
Tourmaline.	Topaz.
Hyacinth.	Heliotrope.

HOPE

Hyacinth.	Hematite.
Opal.	Olivine.
Pearl.	Pyrope.
Emerald.	Essonite.

CHARITY

Cat's-eye.	Carbuncle.
Hyacinth.	Hematite.
Aquamarine.	Amethyst.
Ruby.	Rose quartz.
Iolite.	Idocrase.
Tourmaline.	Topaz.
Yellow sapphire.	Yu (Jade).

GOOD LUCK

Golden beryl.	Garnet.
Opal.	Onyx.
Olivine.	Obsidian.
Diamond.	Dendrite.
Lapis-lazuli.	Labradorite.
Uralian emerald.	Unio pearl.
Cat's-eye.	Carnelian.
Kunzite.	Krokidolite

FOREVER

Fire-opal.	**Flèches d'amour**
Opal.	**Onyx.**
Ruby.	**Rutile.**
Emerald.	**Essonite.**
Vermeille.	**Verd antique.**
Essonite.	**Epidote.**
Rubellite.	**Rose quartz.**

REGARD

Ruby.	Rubellite.
Emerald.	Essonite.
Garnet.	Garnet.
Alexandrite.	Amethyst.
Ruby.	Rock-crystal.
Diamond.	Demantcid.

ZES

Greek, meaning "Mayest thou live."

Zircon.	Zonochlorite.
Emerald.	Essonite.
Sapphire.	Sard.

MIZPAH

Moonstone.	Moldavite.
Indicolite.	Idocrase.
Zircon.	Zonochlorite.
Peridot.	Pyrope.
Asteria.	Aquamarine.
Hyacinth.	Hematite.

FRIENDSHIP

Flèches d'amour	Feldspar.
Ruby.	Rock crystal.
Indicolite.	Idocrase.
Emerald.	Epidote.
Nephrite.	Nicolo.
Diamond.	Diopside.
Sapphire.	Sard.
Hyacinth.	Hematite.
Iolite.	Idocrase.
Pearl.	Pyrite.

DEAREST

Diamond.	Demantoid.
Emerald.	Essonite.
Alexandrite.	Amethyst.
Ruby.	Rubellite.
Essonite.	Epidote.
Sapphire.	Spinel.
Turquoise.	Topaz.

SOUVENIR

Sapphire.	Sunstone.
Opal.	Onyx.
Uralian emerald.	Utahlite.
Vermeille.	Verd antique.
Emerald.	Epidote.
Nephrite.	Nephrite.
Iolite.	Indicolite.
Ruby.	Rock-crystal.

BONHEUR

Beryl.	Bloodstone.
Opal.	Onyx.
Nephrite.	Nephrite.
Hyacinth.	Hematite.
Emerald.	Essonite.
Uralian emerald.	Utahlite.
Ruby.	Rhodonite.

AMITIÉ

Alexandrite.	Almandine.
Moonstone.	Moonstone.
Indicolite.	Indicolite.
Tourmaline.	Topaz.
Idocrase.	Idocrase.
Emerald.	Essonite.

LOVE ME

Lapis-lazuli.	Labrador spar.
Opal.	Onyx.
Vermeille.	Verd antique.
Emerald.	Essonite.
Moonstone.	Moonstone.
Essonite.	Epidote.

A E I

Greek, meaning "forever," "eternity."

Alexandrite.	Almandine.
Emerald.	Essonite.
Indicolite.	Idocrase.

An attractive engagement ring can be formed of a central diamond from which extend the rays of a five-pointed star. Between the rays are set the stones emblematic of the zodiacal sign, of the guardian angel of the month, of the planet control of the hour and also the two stones indicating the initial letter of the two Christian names. This ring is in the form of the mystic Pentagon, the grand symbol of constancy and durability, since the number five is composed of three, which signifies creative power, and two, which typifies the balance, that is, stability.

As, according to the old fancy, the influences due to the light emanations from the planets or fixed stars, or from the combination of the stars in a zodiacal sign, would have a peculiar and more or less intimate connection with the fate of one country rather than of another, an attempt is here made to give a charcteristic stone for each country. In the case of the United States the various gem-stones found within the boundaries of each of the States of the Union are given. That this special influence was exceptionally potent in regard to those born in the countries in question was also taught and hence a national gem would have a greater talismanic power than any other for the natives of each separate country. For those who may feel a certain degree of sympathy for time-honored fancies, and who may perhaps also have a trace of superstition hidden away in some part of their consciousness, one of our State gems would have a similar significance.

GEMS OF COUNTRIES

Alaska	Garnet
Algiers	Coral
Arabia	Pearl
Austria-Hungary	Opal
Belgium	Crystal
Bohemia	Garnet
Bokhara	Lapis-lazuli
Bolivia	Lapis-lazuli
Brazil	Tourmaline (Brazilian emerald)
Burma	Ruby
Canada	Sodalite
Ceylon	Cat's-eye
Chili	Lapis-lazuli
China	Jade
Congo	Dioptase
Denmark	Agate
Egypt	Peridot
England	Diamond
France	Pearl
Germany	Amber
German West Africa	Diamond
Greece	Sapphire
Holland	Diamond
Hungary	Opal
India	Pearl
Ireland	Precious serpentine (Connemara)
Italy	Coral
Japan	Rock-crystal
Korea	Abalone pearl

Madagascar	Morganite
Mexico	Obsidian
Morocco	Coral
New England	Tourmaline
New South Wales	Opal
New Zealand	Jade
Norway-Sweden	Carnelian
Panama	Agate
Persia	Turquoise
Peru	Emerald
Philippines	Pearl
Portugal	Chrysoberyl
Roumania	Amber
Russia	Rhodonite
Sandwich Islands	Olivine
Scotland	Cairngorm (smoky quartz)
Servia	Coral
Siam	Ruby
Sicily	Amber
South Africa	Diamond
Spain	Emerald
Switzerland	Rock-crystal
Turkestan	Jade
Turkey	Turquoise
United States	Sapphire
Uruguay	Amethyst

UNITED STATES STONES

Precious, semi-precious, or gem stones are found in nearly every State of the Union. The most important are enumerated below:

Alabama .... Beryl. blue and yellow; smoky quartz.

Arizona............ Agatized wood, azur-malachite, turquoise, garnet, peridot.

Arkansas.......... Rock-crystal, smoky quartz, agate, diamond, novaculite.

California.......... Agate, benitoite, californite, diamond, gold quartz, tourmaline, abalone pearl, chrysoprase, kunzite, morganite.

Colorado .... Beryl, aquamarine, phenacite, garnet, amethyst, agate, gold quartz, pyrite.
Connecticut .... Beryl, yellow and green; rose quartz, tourmaline.
Delaware .... Pearl.
Florida............ Chalcedony, conch pearl.
Georgia .... Ruby, beryl, amethyst, gold quartz, garnet.
Idaho.............. Opal, agate, obsidian.
Illinois............ Fluorite, pearl.
Indian Territory.... Obsidian, pearl.
Indiana .... Pearl.
Iowa............... Fossil coral, pearl, chalcedony.
Kansas............ Chalcedony.
Kentucky .... Pearl.
Louisiana .... Chalcedony.
Maine .... Tourmaline, beryl, rose quartz, pearl, topaz, amazonite, smoky quartz, rock-crystal.
Maryland .... Beryl, clam-pearl.
Massachusetts....... Beryl.
Michigan........... Agate, hematite.
Minnesota .... Chlorastrolite, thomsonite, agate
Mississippi......... Pearl, chalcedony.
Missouri .... Pearl, fluorite, pyrite.
Montana .... Sapphire, beryl, smoky quartz, agate, amethyst, agatized wood, obsidian.
Nebraska........... Chalcedony, pearl.
Nevada .... Gold quartz, rock-crystal.
New Hampshire .... Beryl, rock-crystal, garnet.
New Jersey........ Fowlerite, willemite, prehnite, smoky quartz, agate, pearl.
New Mexico........ Turquoise, garnet, obsidian, peridot, rock-crystal.
New York .... Beryl, brown tourmaline, rose quartz, fresh-water pearl, clam-pearl, chondrodite.
North Carolina ..... Aquamarine, beryl, emerald, almandite garnet, rhodolite, pyrope garnet, diamond, cyanite, hiddenite, amethyst, ruby, sapphire, smoky quartz, rock-crystal, rutile.
North Dakota ...... Chalcedony, agate.
Ohio............... Fossil coral, chalcedony.
Oregon............. Agate, obsidian, hydrolite.

Pennsylvania.......**Amethyst, beryl, sunstone, moonstone, amazonite, almandite garnet, pyrope garnet, rutile.**
Rhode Island.......**Hornblende in quartz, amethyst, rock-crystal.**
South Carolina.....**Beryl, smoky quartz, rock-crystal.**
South Dakota.......**Quartzite, beryl, agate.**
Tennessee..........**Pearl.**
Texas.............**Beryl, pearl, tourmaline.**
Utah...............**Topaz, garnet.**
Virginia............**Amethyst, spessarite, garnet, beryl, moonstone, staurolite, allanite.**
Vermont............**Beryl, pearl.**
Washington.........**Pearl, agate.**
West Virginia......**Rock-crystal.**
Wisconsin..........**Agate, pearl.**
Wyoming...........**Moss-agate, agate.**

INSCRIPTION ON A SMALL PIECE OF LIMESTONE, IN CURSIVE EGYPTIAN WRITING.

It dates from about 1600 B.C., the period of the Ebers Papyrus, and gives directions for preparing certain remedies from precious stones. While the interpretation of this text offers considerable difficulty, one version finds in it the statement that lapis-lazuli—the "sapphire" of the ancients—was used for the wealthy, and malachite for those of limited means. Professor Oefele conjectures that the disease to be treated was hysteria. Munch Collection, Metropolitan Museum of Art, New York.

V

On the Therapeutic Use of Precious and Semi-Precious Stones

THE medicinal use of precious stones may be traced back to very ancient times. It has been conjectured that their employment for such purposes was introduced to Europe from India, whence many of the stones were derived. Nevertheless, the earliest evidence we have rather points to Egypt as the source, and, indeed, it appears that in early Egyptian times the chemical constituents of the stones were much more rationally considered than at a later period in Europe. The Ebers Papyrus, for instance, recommends the use of certain astringent substances, such as lapis-lazuli, as ingredients of eye-salves, and hematite, an iron oxide, was used for checking hemorrhages and for reducing inflammations. Little by little, however, superstition associated certain special virtues with the color and quality of precious stones, and their virtues were thought to be greatly enhanced by engraving on them the image of some god, or of some object symbolizing certain of the activities of nature. Later still, the science of astrology, most highly developed in Assyria and Babylonia, was brought into combination with the various superstitions above indicated, so that the image was believed to have much greater efficacy if the engraving were executed when the sun was in a certain constellation or when the moon or some one of the planets was in the ascendant at the time.

If we exclude certain fragmentary notices in Egyptian literature—notably the statements in the Ebers Papyrus—and the very uncertain sources in Hindu literature, the earliest authority for this branch of the subject is the Natural History of Pliny. In this connection, however, it is only just to call attention to a fact which has been often ignored—namely, that Pliny himself had very little faith in the teachings of the "magi," as he calls them, in regard to the superstitious use of gems for the prevention or cure of diseases; indeed, he seems to have been almost as sceptical in his attitude as many modern writers, for certain quite recent authorities still credit amber and a few other mineral substances with therapeutic effects other than those which can be explained by the known action of their chemical constituents. Still, Pliny yielded so far to the taste of his time as to preserve for us many of the statements of earlier writers on the subject, naming them in most cases and so enabling us to form some idea of the character of this pseudo-science in the Roman world in the first century of our era. With the gradual decay of ancient learning, the less valuable elements of popular belief came more and more into the foreground, and the old superstitions were freely copied by successive authors, each of whom felt called upon to add something new on his own account. This explains much of the confusion that reigns in regard to the attribution of special virtues to the different stones, for the wider the reading of the author the greater became the number of virtues attributed to each separate stone, until, at last, we might almost say that each and every precious stone could be used for the cure of all diseases. Nevertheless, it is comparatively easy to see that either the color or constitution of the stone originally indicated its use for this or that disease.

A distinction is often made between the talismanic

qualities of precious stones for the cure or prevention of disease and the properly medicinal use of them as mineral substances. In the former case the effect was attained by merely wearing them on the person, while in the latter case they were reduced to a powder, which was dissolved as far as possible in water or some other liquid and then taken internally. As, however, the end to be attained is the same whether the stone be worn or taken internally as a powder or liquid, it seems more logical to treat of both these methods of therapeutic use together, reserving for the chapter on the talismanic use of gems only their employment to avert misfortunes other than those caused by disease, and their influence in the procuring of wealth, honors, and happiness for their wearers.

The belief in the curative properties of precious stones was at one time universal among all those to whom gems were known. When we read to-day of the various ills that were supposed to be cured by the use of these gems, we find it difficult to understand what process of thought could have suggested the idea of employing such ineffectual remedies. It is true that the constituents of certain stones can be absorbed by the human body and have a definite effect upon it, but the greater part of the elements are so combined that they cannot be assimilated, and they pass through the system without producing any apparent effect.

In ancient and medieval times, however, other than chemical agencies were supposed to be efficient in the cure of diseases, and the primitive animistic conception of the cause of illness, and hence of the therapeutics of disease, long held sway among those who practised the medical art. Remedies were prized because of their rarity, and also because it was believed that certain spiritual or planetary influences had aided in their production and were latent in them. Besides this, the symbolism of color played a very important part in recommending the use of particular stones for special diseases. This may be noted in the case of the red or reddish stones, such as the ruby, spinel, garnet, carnelian, bloodstone, etc. These were thought to be sovereign remedies for hemorrhages of all kinds, as well as for all inflammatory diseases; they were also believed to exercise a calming influence and to remove anger and discord. The red hue of these stones was supposed to indicate their fitness for such use, upon the principle *similia similibus curantur*. In the same way yellow stones were prescribed for the cure of bilious disorders, for jaundice in all its forms and for other diseases of the liver.

The use of green stones to relieve diseases of the eye was evidently suggested by the beneficial influence exerted by this color upon the sight. The verdant emerald represented the beautiful green fields, upon which the tired eye rests so willingly, and which exert such a soothing influence upon the sight when it has been unduly strained or fatigued. One of the earliest, probably the very earliest reference in Greek writings to the therapeutic value of gems, appears in the works of Theophrastus, who wrote in the third century before Christ. Here we are told of the beneficial effect exercised by the emerald upon the eyes.

The sapphire, the lapis-lazuli, and other blue stones, with a hue resembling the blue of the heavens, were believed to exert a tonic influence, and were supposed to counteract the wiles of the spirits of darkness and procure the aid and favor of the spirits of light and wisdom. These gems were usually looked upon as emblems of chastity, and for this reason the sapphire came to be

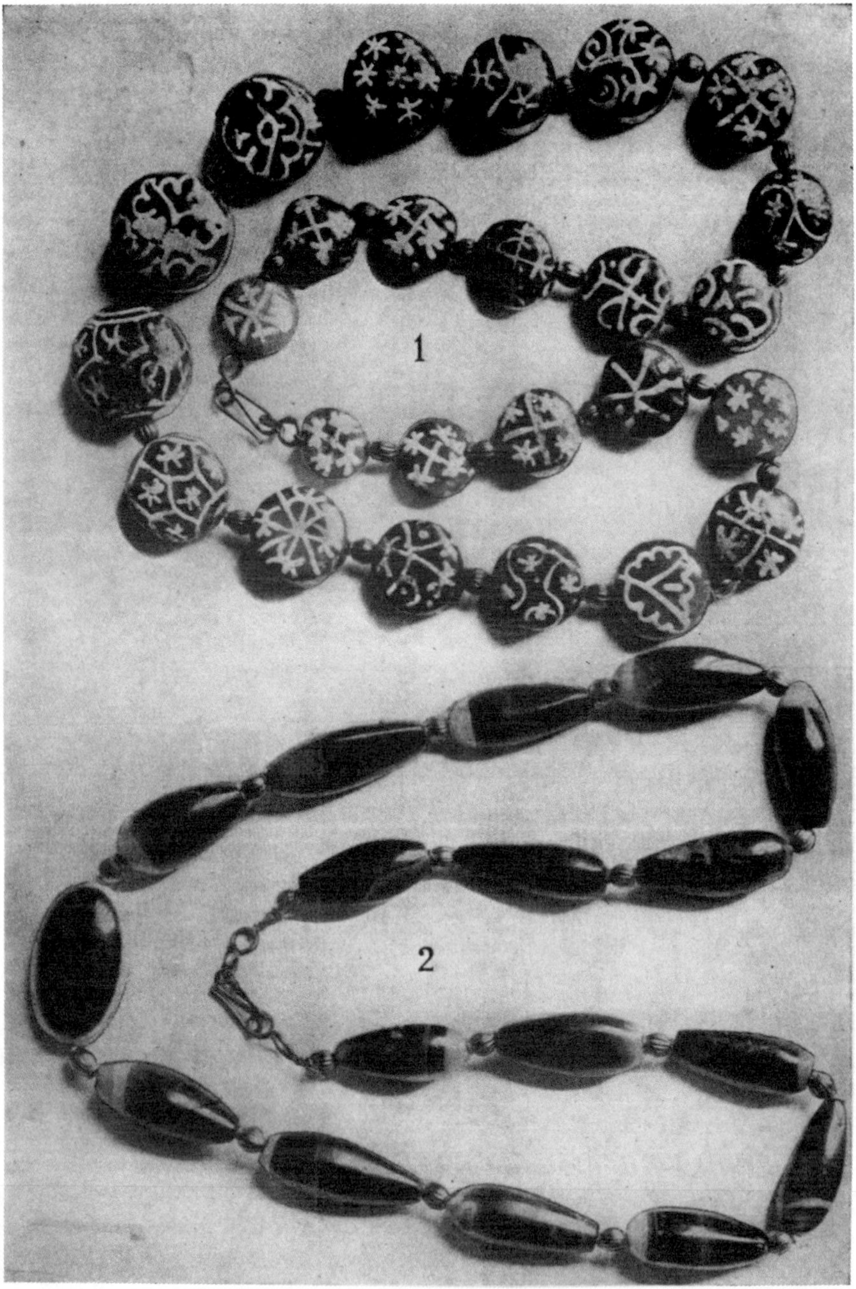

1. Necklace of carnelian beads. Persian. The decoration is made with carbonate of lime and fixed by firing. Charms against the Evil Eye.
2. Necklace of onyx beads. Early Christian.

regarded as especially appropriate for use in ecclesiastical rings. Among purple stones, the amethyst is particularly noteworthy. The well-known belief that this gem counteracted the effects of undue indulgence in intoxicating beverages is indicated by its name, derived from μεθύω — "to be intoxicated," and the privative α, the name thus signifying the "sobering" gem. It is not unlikely that a fancied resemblance between the prevailing hue of these stones and that of certain kinds of wine first gave rise to the name and to the idea of the peculiar virtues of the amethyst.

We have mentioned only a few of the more obvious analogies suggested by the color of gems, and we might be tempted to cite many others were it not that symbolism is always treacherous ground, since there is practically no limit to the correspondences that may be found between sensuous impressions and ideas.

One great difficulty which besets any one who is trying to find a clue to guide him through the labyrinth of the medical affinities of gems is the fact that there was, from an early period, a tendency to attribute the virtues of one gem to another, probably owing to the commercial instinct which urged the dealer to praise his wares in every possible way, so that no part of his stock should fail to find a purchaser. This tendency is especially marked in the old Hindu Lapidaries, wherein it is almost impossible to find any differentiation of the stones in respect to their curative or talismanic virtues. Only the condition and perfection of the gems are made the criterion of their worth. Any given stone, if perfect, was a source of all blessings to the wearer and possessed all remedial powers, while a defective stone, or one lacking the proper lustre or color, was destined to be a source of untold misfortune to the owner.

The European writers on the medical properties of precious stones were influenced by quite different considerations; their chief aim was to represent each stone, regarded simply as a mineral substance, as being the abode of the greatest possible number of curative properties. Indeed, many of the most highly recommended electuaries contained all kinds of stones, as though the effect to be produced did not depend upon the qualities of any single stone, or class of stones, but rather upon the quantity used. In Arnobio's "Tesoro delle Gioie,"[1] we have a receipt for the composition of "the most noble electuary of jacinth." This contains jacinth, emerald, sapphire, topaz, garnet, pearl, ruby, white and red coral, and amber, as well as many animal and vegetable substances, in all, thirty-four ingredients. It would indeed seem that a good dose of such a mixture should have provided a cure for "all the ills that flesh is heir to," by the simple and effective means of removing the unhappy patient to a better world.

Treating of the metallic affinities of precious stones, Paracelsus (1493–1541) affirmed that the emerald was a copper stone; the carbuncle and the jasper were golden stones; the ruby and the chalcedony, silver stones. The "white sapphire" (corundum) was a stone of Jupiter, while the jacinth was a mercurial stone. Powdered jacinth mixed with an equal quantity of laudanum was recommended as a remedy for fevers resulting from "putrefaction of the air or water." This illustrates the custom of combining an inefficacious material, such as the powder of a precious stone, with another possessing genuine remedial virtue, the name of the stone appealing to the popular superstitions regarding its thera-

[1] Venice, 1602, p. 254.

peutic powers, and thus rendering the preparation more acceptable.[2]

It is related by Plutarch that when Pericles was dying of the plague, he showed to one of his friends, who was visiting him, an amulet suspended from his neck. This had been given to Pericles by the women of his household, and Plutarch cites the instance as a proof that even the strongest minds will at certain times yield to the influence of superstition.[3]

There were sceptics in ancient times who put no faith in the popular superstitions as to the curative powers of precious stones. Eusebius (ca. 264–ca. 349), in his oration on the Emperor Constantine the Great (272–337), says:[4]

> He held that the varieties of stones so greatly admired were useless and ineffective things. They possessed no other qualities than their natural ones, and hence no efficacy to hold evils aloof; for what power can such things have either to cure disease or to avert death? Nevertheless, although he well knew this, he was in no wise opposed to their use simply as ornaments by his subjects.

The Middle High German didactic poem on precious stones, composed by Volmar, or Volamar, about 1250, appears to have been written as a rejoinder to a satirical poem, the work of a writer called the "Stricker" (rascal). What chiefly aroused Volmar's wrath was the fact that this irreverent personage dared to assert that a piece of

---

[2] "The Hermetic and Alchemical writings of Aureolus Philippus Theophrastus Bombast of Hohenheim, called Paracelsus the Great," trans. by Arthur Edward Waite, London, 1894, Vol. I, pp. 14, 225, Vol. II, p. 218.

[3] Plutarchi, "Vitæ," ed. Sinteris, Lipsiæ, 1884, p. 339; Pericles, 38.

[4] Eusebii Pamphili, "De laudibus Constantini," cap. v; in Eusebii, "Opera Omnia," ed. Migne, Parisiis, 1857, cols. 1337, 1340; Patrologiæ Græcæ, vol. xx.

colored glass set in a ring looked just as well and possessed the same virtues as a genuine precious stone of the same color. Volmar does not mince matters, and roundly declares that whoever should kill the man who wrote thus would do no sinful act. While we can scarcely recommend such drastic action, we must admit that we feel a little sympathy with the medieval champion of genuine stones against imitations.

A most interesting item recording one phase of a great tyrant's character is reported by Sir Jerome Horsey, who was entrusted with messages to and from Elizabeth of England and Ivan the Terrible of Russia. He gives, in his "Travels," a graphic recital of an interview with Ivan just before the latter's death in 1584. We retain the archaic spelling as it is reproduced in the Hakluyt publication from the original manuscript. Writing of Ivan, Horsey says: [5]

Carried every daye in his chair into his treasure. One daye the prince beckoned me to follow. I strode emonge the rest venturously, and heard him call for som precious stones and jewells. Told the prince and nobles present before and aboute him the virtue of such and such, which I observed, and do pray I may a littell degress to declare for my own memorie sake.

"The load-stone you all know hath great and hidden vertue, without which the seas that compas the world ar not navigable, nor the bounds nor circles of the earth cannot be knowen. Mahomett, the Percians proffit, his tombe of steell hangs in their Repatta at Darbent most miraculously"—Caused the waiters to bringe a chaine of nedells towched by his load-stone, hanged all one by the other.—"This faire currell (coral) and this faire turcas you see; take in your hand; of his natur arr orient coullers; put them on my hand and arm. I am poisoned with disease: you see they shewe their virtue by the chainge of their pure culler into pall: declares my death. Reach owt my staff roiall; an unicorns horn garnished with verie fare diomondes, rubies,

[5] The Travels of Sir Jerome Horsey, Hakluyt Society, London, 1856, pp. 199, 200.

saphiers, emeralls and other precious stones that ar rich in vallew; cost 70 thousand marckes sterlinge of David Gower from the fowlkers of Ousborghe.[6] Seek owt for som spiders." Caused his phiziccians, Johannes Lloff, to scrape a circle thereof upon the tabell; putt within it one spider and so one other and died, and some other without that ran alive apace from it.—"It is too late, it will not preserve me. Behold these precious stones. This diomond is the orients richest and most precious of all other. I never affected it; yt restroyns furie and luxurie and abstinacie and chasticie; the least parcell of it in powder will poysen a horse geaven to drinck, much more a man." Poynts at the ruby. "Oh! this is most comfortable to the hart, braine, vigar and memorie of man, clarifies congelled and corrupt bloud."—Then at the emerald.—"The natur of the reyn-bowe; this precious stone is an enemye to uncleanness. The saphier I greatlie delight in; yt preserves and increaseth courage, joies the hart, pleasinge to all the vitall sensis, precious and verie soveraigne for the eys, clears the sight, takes awaye bloudshott and streingthens the mussells and strings thereof."—Then takes the onex in hand.—"All these are Gods wonderfull guifts, secreats in natur, and yet revells [reveals] them to mans use and contemplacion, as frendes to grace and vertue and enymies to vice. I fainte, carie me awaye till an other tyme."

Some believed that when precious stones were worn to relieve or prevent disease, it was important that the different stones should be worn on different parts of the body. According to one authority, the jacinth should be worn on the neck; the diamond, on the left arm; the sapphire, on the ring-finger; the emerald, or the jacinth, on the index-finger; and the ruby or turquoise, on either the index-finger or the little finger.[7] There is, however, little reason to assume that these rules were generally known and observed.

That precious stones not only appealed to the eye by

[6] The Fuggers of Augsburg, the jeweller bankers of the 15th and 16th centuries.

[7] Wolffii, "Curiosus amuletorum scrutator," Francofurti et Lipsiæ, 1692, p. 363; citing Rodolphus Goclenius (De peste, p. 70).

their beautiful colors, but also possessed a fragrant odor, was one of the many fanciful ideas regarding them. If we could believe the following circumstantial account, this was once experimentally proved:[8]

> When precious stones are to be used in medicine, they must be pulverized until they are reduced to a powder so fine that it will not grate under the teeth, or, in the words of Galen, this powder must be as impalpable "as that which is blown into the eyes." Since this trituration is not usually operated with sufficient care by the apothecaries, I begged a medical student, who was lodging with me, to pass an entire month in grinding some of these stones. I gave him emeralds, jacinths, sapphires, rubies, and pearls, an ounce of each kind. As these stones were rough and whole, he first crushed them a little in a well-polished iron mortar, using a pestle of the same metal; afterward he employed a pestle and mortar of glass, devoting several hours each day to this work. At the end of about three weeks, his room, which was rather large, became redolent with a perfume, agreeable both from its variety and sweetness. This odor, which much resembled that of March violets, lingered in the room for more than three days. There was nothing in the room to produce it, so that it certainly proceeded from the powder of precious stones.

Diamond

Of the many medicinal virtues attributed to the diamond, one of the most noteworthy is that of an antidote for poisons. Strangely enough, the belief in its efficacy in this respect was coupled with the idea that the stone in itself was a deadly poison. The origin of this latter fancy must be sought in the tradition that the place wherein the diamonds were generated—"in the land where it is six months day and six months night"—was guarded by venomous creatures who, in passing over the stones, were wounded by the sharp points of the crystals,

---

[8] Olaus Borrichius, in the Collection Académique, Paris, 1757, tome iv, p. 338.

and thus embued the stones with some of their venom.[9] The attribution of curative properties in case of poisoning arose from association of ideas. The Lapidario of Alfonso X recommends the diamond for diseases of the bladder; it adds, however, that this stone should be used only in desperate cases.

The diamond was also believed to afford protection from plague or pestilence, and a proof of its powers in this direction was found in the fact that the plague first attacked the poorer classes, sparing the rich, who could afford to adorn themselves with diamonds. Naturally, in common with other precious stones, this brilliant gem was supposed to cure many diseases. Marbodus[10] tells us that it was even a cure for insanity.

In the Babylonian Talmud we read of a marvellous precious stone belonging to Abraham. This was perhaps a diamond, or possibly a pearl; the accounts vary, and the same word is often used to designate "precious stone" and "pearl." The following version represents it to be a diamond:[11]

R. Simeon, ben Johanan said: "A diamond was hanging on Abraham's neck, and when a sick man looked upon it he was cured. And when Abraham passed away, the Lord sealed it in the planet of the sun."

The Hindus believed that it was extremely dangerous to use diamonds of inferior quality for curative purposes, as they would not only fail to remedy the disease for which they were prescribed, but might cause lameness,

---

[9] Lapidario del Rey D. Alfonso X, Codice Original, Madrid, 1881, f. xi.

[10] "De lapidibus," Friburgi, 1531, f. 8.

[11] New edition of the Babylonian Talmud, ed. and trans. by Michael L. Rodkinson, vol. v (xiii), Baba Barat, New York, 1902, p. 53. See also Beer, "Leben Abraham's," Leipzig, 1859, p. 79.

jaundice, pleurisy, and even leprosy. As to the use of diamonds of good quality, very explicit directions are given. On some day regarded as auspicious for the operation, the stone was to be dipped in the juice of the *kantakára* (*Solanum jaquiri*) and subjected for a whole night to the heat of a fire made by dried pieces of the dung of a cow or of a buffalo. In the morning it was to be immersed in cow's urine and again subjected to fire. These processes were to be repeated for seven days, at the end of which term the diamond could be regarded as purified. After this the stone was to be buried in a paste of certain leguminous seeds mixed with asafœtida and rock salt. Herein it was to be heated twenty-one successive times, when it would be reduced to ashes. If these ashes were then dissolved in some liquid, the potion would "conduce to longevity, general development of the body, strength, energy, beauty of complexion, and happiness," giving an adamantine strength to the limbs.[12]

An Austrian nobleman, who for a long time had not been able to sleep without having terrible dreams, was immediately cured by wearing a small diamond set in gold on his arm, so that the stone came in contact with his skin.[13]

The fact that in this case, as in many others, the stone was required to touch the skin, proves that the effect supposed to be produced was not altogether magical, but in the nature of a physical emanation from the stone to the body of the wearer.

We are told that when Pope Clement VII was seized by his last illness, in 1534, his physicians resorted to

---

[12] Surindro Mohun Tagore, "Mani Málá," Pt. I, Calcutta, 1879, pp. 137, 139, 141.

[13] Andrea Spigello, "De semitert."; cited in Gimma, "Della Storia naturale delle gemme," Napoli, 1730, vol. i, p. 208.

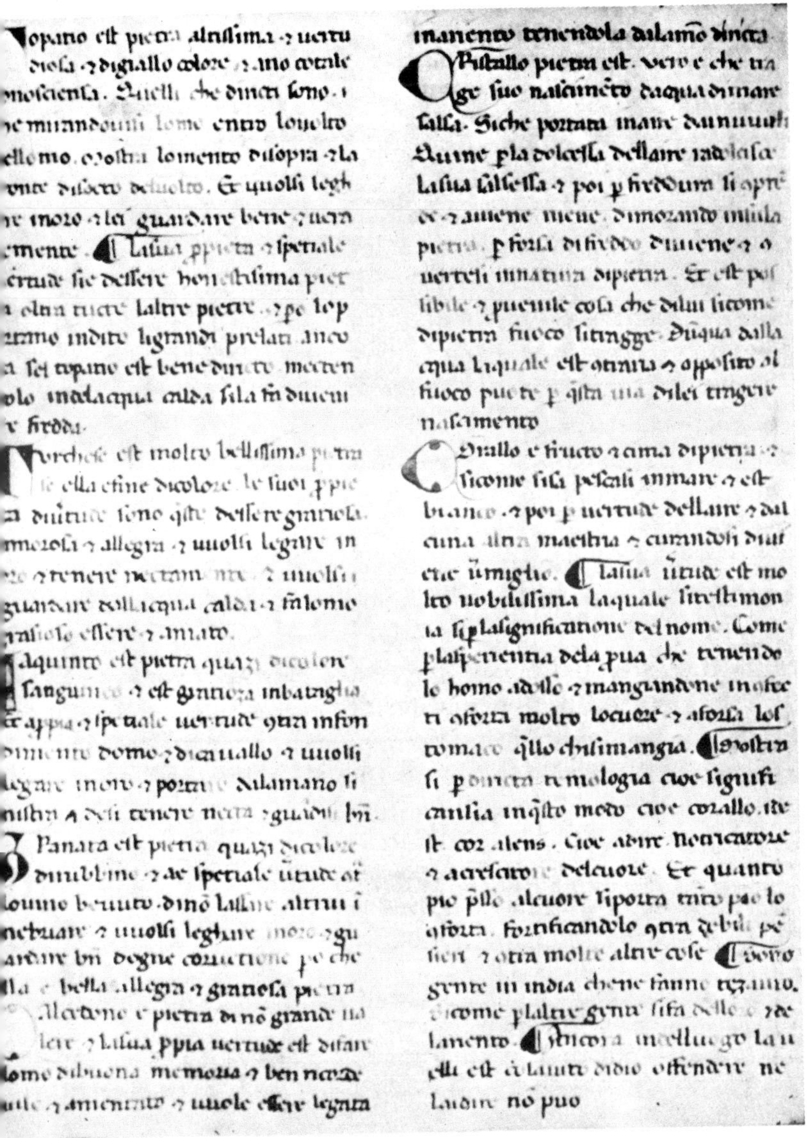

Facsimile page of Italian vellum manuscript treatise of the virtues of gems. Italian MS. the Fourteenth Century in author's library.
Treating of Topaz, Turquoise, Jacinth, Garnet, Chalcedony, Rock-crystal, Coral.

powders composed of various precious stones. In the space of fourteen days they are asserted to have given the pope forty thousand ducats' worth of these stones, a single dose costing as much as three thousand ducats. The most costly remedy of all was a diamond administered to him at Marseilles. Unfortunately, this lavish expenditure was of no avail; indeed, according to our modern science, the remedies might have sufficed to end the pope's life, without the help of his disease.[14]

The old fancy that the diamond grew dark in the presence of poison is explained by the Italian physician Gonelli as caused by minute and tenuous particles which emanated from the poison, impinged upon the surface of the diamond, and, unable to penetrate its dense mass, accumulated on the surface, thus producing a superficial discoloration. The diamond, being a cold substance, may have condensed moisture from the body, and the one suffering from the poison may have emitted exudations. But this elaborate explanation of a phenomenon which never existed except in the imagination of those who related it is characteristic of Gonelli, who was always ready to elucidate in some similar way any of the marvels recounted in regard to precious stones.[15]

Emerald

The emerald was employed as an antidote for poisons and for poisoned wounds, as well as against demoniacal possession.[16] If worn on the neck it was said to cure the

[14] Raumer, "Historisches Taschenbuch," I Ser., vol. vi, Leipzig, 1835, p. 370.

[15] Josephi Gonelli, "Thesaurus philosophicus, seu de gemmis," Neapoli, 1702, pp. 76, 77.

[16] Lapidario del Rey D. Alfonso X, Codice Original, Madrid, 1881, f. xv.

"semitertian" fever and epilepsy.[17] The use of the emerald to rest and relieve the eye is the only remedial use of a precious stone mentioned by Theophrastus in his treatise on gems, written in the third century B.C. Alluding to its powers as an antidote for poisons, Rueus asserts [18] that if the weight of eighty barley-corns of its powder were given to one dying from the effects of poison, the dose would save his life. The Arabs prized emeralds highly for this purpose, and Abenzoar states that, having once taken a poisonous herb, he placed an emerald in his mouth and applied another to his stomach, whereupon he was entirely cured.[19]

A certain cure for dysentery also was to wear an emerald suspended so that it touched the abdomen and to place another emerald in the mouth. Michaele Paschali, a learned Spanish physician of the sixteenth century, declared that he had effected a cure of the disease by means of the emerald in the case of Juan de Mendoza, a Spanish grandee, and Wolfgang Gabelchover, of Calw, in Würtemberg, writing in 1603, asserts that he had often tested the virtues of the emerald in cases of dysentery and with invariable success.[20]

It speaks not a little for the beauty of the emerald that so good a judge of precious stones as Pliny should have pronounced this gem to be the only one that delighted the eye without fatiguing it, adding that when the vision was wearied by gazing intently at other objects, it gained renewed strength by viewing an emerald. So general in the early centuries of our era was the persuasion that

---

[17] Marbodus, l. c., f. 48.

[18] Rueus, l. c., p. 36.

[19] Morales, "De las piedras preciosas," Valladolid, 1604, f. 101.

[20] Andreæ Bacci, "De gemmis et lapidibus pretiosis," Francofurti, 1603, pp. 63, 64 (annotation of Gabelchover to his Latin version).

the pure green hue of emeralds aided the eyesight, that gem engravers are said to have kept some of them on their work-tables, so as to be able to look at the stones from time to time and thus relieve the eye-strain caused by close application to their delicate task.[21]

Psellus says that a cataplasm made of emeralds was of help to those suffering from leprosy; he adds that if pulverized and taken in water they would check hemorrhages.[22] They were especially commended for use as amulets to be hung on the necks of children, as they were believed to ward off and prevent epilepsy. If, however, the violence of the disease was such that it could not be overcome by the stone, the latter would break.[23] Hermes Trismegistus says the emerald cures ophthalmia and hemorrhages. The great Hermes must have had a special preference for this stone, since his treatise on chemistry (*peri chemeias*) is said to have been found inscribed on an emerald.[24]

By the Hindu physicians of the thirteenth century the emerald was considered to be a good laxative. It cured dysentery, diminished the secretion of bile, and stimulated the appetite. In short, it promoted bodily health and destroyed demoniacal influences. In the curious phrase of the school the emerald was "cold and sweet."[25]

Teifashi (1242 A.D.) believed that the emerald was a

---

[21] Plinii, "Naturalis historia," lib. xxxvii, cap. 16.

[22] Psellus, "De lapidum virtutibus," Lug. Bat., 1745, p. 32.

[23] Johannis Braunii, "De Vestitu sacerd. Heb.," Amstel., 1680, p. 659.

[24] From an old book the title-page of which reads: "In hoc volumine de Alchemia," etc., Norimberghe, 1541, p. 363.

[25] Garbe, "Die indische Mineralien; Naharari's Rajanighantu, Varga xiii," Leipzig, 1882, p. 76.

cure for hæmoptysis and for dysentery if it were worn over the liver of the person affected; to cure gastric troubles, the stone was to be laid upon the stomach. Furthermore, the wearer was protected from the attacks of venomous creatures, and evil spirits were driven from the place where emeralds were kept.[26] The direction to place the stone on the affected part, a recommendation often met with in the treatises on the therapeutic use of ornamental stones, shows that these were believed to send forth emanations of subtle power. Probably enough, the brilliant play of reflected light which proceeds from many of these gems suggested the idea that they radiated a certain curative energy. This theory need not surprise us, for, although it is altogether fanciful in the case of the diamond, ruby, emerald, etc., the newly discovered substance, radium, really possesses the active properties ascribed by old writers to precious stones.

Jade

A stone the therapeutic quality of which was specialized is the jade or nephrite. Strange to say, although there are very few places where this mineral can now be obtained,—the chief sources of supply being the province of Khotan in Turkistan and New Zealand,—in prehistoric times the stone must have been found in many different localities, since axe-heads and other artefacts of jade have been discovered in many lands both of the old and new world.

When the Spaniards discovered and explored the southern part of the American continent, they came across numerous native ornaments and amulets made of jade (jadeite) and brought many of these with them to

---

[26] Teifashi, "Fior di pensieri sulle pietre preziose," Ital. trans. by Antonio Raineri, Firenzi, 1818, p. 20.

Europe. The name jade is derived from the Spanish designation, *piedra de hijada,* meaning literally "stone of the flank." which is said to have been bestowed on the stone because the Indians used it for all diseases of the kidneys. The name nephrite owes its origin to the same idea. In ancient times jade appears to have been looked upon as a great aid in parturition, and many ingenious conjectures have been advanced as to the connection between this belief and the form of some of the prehistoric objects made of this material. Whether the Spaniards really learned from the Indians that the stone was especially adapted to cure renal diseases, or whether they only suggested this special and peculiar virtue in order to give an enhanced value to their jade ornaments, is a question not easily answered.

An early notice of jade as a remedial agent appears in Sir Walter Raleigh's account of his travels in Guiana. Treating of a people of "Amazons" said to dwell in the interior of the country, Raleigh says:[27]

> These Amazones have likewise great store of these plates of golde, which they recover by exchange, chiefly for a kinde of greene stone, which the Spaniards call Piedras Hijadas, and we use for spleene stones and for the disease of the stone we also esteeme them: of these I saw divers in Guiana, and commonly every King or *Casique* hath one, which theire wives for the most part weare, and they esteeme them as great jewels.

By the middle of the seventeenth century the curative powers of jade for the various forms of calculi was very generally admitted. A singular instance is offered us in one of Voiture's letters. He was a great sufferer from "the stone" and he had received, from a Mademoiselle Paulet, a beautiful jade bracelet. Gratefully acknowl-

[27] "The Discovery of the Large, Rich, and Beautiful Empire of Guiana," London, 1848, p. 29, Hakluyt Pub. Originally published in 1596.

edging the receipt of this peculiar gift, he expresses himself in the following frank way, a mixture of indelicacy and gallantry that seems strange to us: "If the stones you have given me do not break mine, they will at least make me bear my sufferings patiently; and it seems to me that I ought not to complain of my colic, since it has procured me this happiness." The name used for jade by Voiture, "*l'éjade*," supplied a missing link in the derivation of our name jade from the Spanish *hijada*. When the lady's gift was received by Voiture, some friends chanced to be present, and they were disposed to regard it as a token of love until he assured them that it was only a remedy. It appears that Mlle. Paulet was a fellow sufferer, and, alluding to this, Voiture writes: "On this occasion the jade had for you an effect you did not expect from it, and its virtue defended your own."[28]

Renal calculi and poetry do not seem to have much in common, but the following lines freely rendered from an old Italian poem on the subject by Ciri de Pers show that even this unpromising theme is susceptible of poetic treatment:[29]

> "Other white stones serve to mark happy days,
> But mine do mark days full of pain and gloom.
> To build a palace, or a temple fair,
> Stones should be used; but mine do serve
> To wreck the fleshly temple of my soul.
>
> . . . .
>
> Well do I know that Death doth whet his glaive
> Upon these stones, and that the marble white
> That grows in me is there to form my tomb."

---

[28] Lettres de Voiture, ed. by Octave Uzanne, Paris, 1880, vol. i, p. 66, Letter XXIII.

[29] Josephi Gonnelli, Thesaurus philosophicus, seu de gemmis," Neapoli, 1702, pp. 157, 158.

As jade was and still is the most favored stone in China, although never found within the boundaries of China proper, it was very naturally accorded wonderful medical virtues. An old Chinese encyclopedia, the work of Li She Chan, and presented by him to the emperor Wan Lih of the Ming dynasty, in 1596, contains many interesting notices of jade. When reduced to a powder of the size of rice grains it strengthened the lungs, the heart, and the vocal organs, and prolonged life, more especially if gold and silver were added to the jade powder. Another, and certainly a pleasanter way of absorbing this precious mineral, was to drink what was enthusiastically called the "divine liquor of jade." To concoct this elixir equal parts of jade, rice, and dew-water were put into a copper pot and boiled, the resultant liquid being carefully filtered. This mixture was said to strengthen the muscles and make them supple, to harden the bones, to calm the mind, to enrich the flesh, and to purify the blood. Whoever took it for a long space of time ceased to suffer from either heat or cold and no longer felt either hunger or thirst.

Galen (b. ca. 130 A.D.) wrote thus of the green jasper:[30]

> Some have testified to a virtue in certain stones, and this is true of the green jasper, that is to say, this stone aids the stomach and navel by contact. And some, therefore, set the stone in rings and engrave on it a dragon surrounded by rays, according to what King Nechepsos has transmitted to posterity in the fourteenth book (of his works). Indeed, I myself have thoroughly tested this stone, for I hung a necklace composed of them about my neck so that they touched the navel, and I received not less benefit from them than I would had they borne the engraving of which Nechepsos wrote.

[30] Claudii Galeni, "De simplic. medicament., etc.," lib. ix, cap. 19. "Opera Omnia," ed. C. G. Kühn, Lipsiæ, 1826, vol. xii, p. 207. See also Duffield Osborne, "Engraved Gems," New York, 1912, pp. 138, 139.

Ruby

Sanskrit medical literature as represented by Naharari, a physician of Cashmere, who wrote in the thirteenth century, finds in the ruby a valuable remedy for flatulency and biliousness. Moreover, aside from these special uses, an elixir of great potency could be made from rubies by those who properly understood the employment of precious stones in the compounding of medicines.[31] This famous "ruby elixir" may have had little in common with the stone except its color, as such remedies were generally said to have been made by some secret and mysterious process, in the course of which all material evidence of the presence of any precious stone or stones completely disappeared.

Sapphire

One of the earliest specimens of English literature, William Langley's "Vision of William concerning Piers the Plowman" (written about 1377), contains a mention of the sapphire as a cure for disease:[32]

> I looked on my left half as þe lady me taughte
> And was war of a woman wortheli yeclothed,
> Purfiled with pelure[33] þe finest vpon erthe,
> Y-crowned with a corone þe kyng hath none better.
> Fetislich[34] hir fyngres were fretted[35] with gold wyre,

---

[31] Garbe, "Die indische Mineralien"; Naharari's "Rajanighantu," Varga XIII, Leipzig, 1882, p. 70.

[32] The Vision of William Concerning Piers the Plowman, by William Langley (or Langland). Ed. by Rev. Walter W. Skeat, Oxford, 1881, p. 16. Passus II, lines 8–15.

[33] Trimmed with fur.

[34] Handsomely.

[35] Adorned.

> And þere-on red rubyes as red as any glede,[36]
> And diamants of derrest pris, and double manere safferes,
> Orientales and ewages [37] enuenymes [38] to destroye.

Among the rich gifts offered at the shrine of St. Erkinwald, in Old Saint Paul's, was a sapphire given in 1391 by Richard Preston, "a citizen and grocer of London." He stipulated that the stone should be kept at the shrine for the cure of diseases of the eyes, and that proclamation should be made of its remedial virtues. St. Erkinwald was the son of Offa, King of the East Saxons, and was converted to Christianity by Melittus, the first bishop of London. In 675 A.D. he himself became bishop of London, being the third to attain that rank after the death of Melittus. His body was interred in the cathedral, and his shrine, which was richly embellished during the reign of Edward III (1327–1377), received many valuable donations.[39]

The usefulness of the sapphire as an eyestone for the removal of all impurities or foreign bodies from the eye is noted by Albertus Magnus, who writes that he had seen it employed for this purpose. He adds that when a sapphire was used in this way it should be dipped in cold water both before and after the operation.[40] This was probably not so much to make the stone colder to the touch as to cleanse it, certainly a very necessary proceeding when the same stone was used by many persons suffering from contagious diseases of the eyes.

---

[36] Burning coal.

[37] Aquamarines.

[38] Poisons.

[39] Dugdale, "History of Saint Paul's Cathedral in London," London, 1818, vol. i, pp. 15, 16. First edition published in 1658.

[40] Alberti Magni, "Opera omnia," ed. Borgnet, Paris, 1890, vol. v, p. 44.

Richard Preston's sapphire appears to have been only one of a class regarded as having special virtue to cure diseased eyes, as is shown by the existence of various other similar sapphires in different parts of Europe. It is not very easy to determine the precise reason—if there be one—which rendered any single sapphire more useful than another in this respect. An entry in the inventory of Charles V notes "an oval Oriental sapphire for touching the eyes, set in a band of gold."[41] Possibly the fact that a particular gem of this kind was used remedially, and was not set for wear as an ornament, may have been the only cause for a belief in its special virtue.

That the sapphire should have been regarded as especially valuable for the cure of eye diseases serves to illustrate the wide-reaching and persistent influence of Egyptian thought, and the curious transformations through which an originally reasonable idea may pass in the course of time. We have already noted that the sapphire of the ancients was our lapis-lazuli, and in the Ebers Papyrus lapis-lazuli is given as one of the ingredients of an eye-wash. This ingredient is believed to have originally been the oxide of copper sometimes called lapis Armenus, a material possessing marked astringent properties, and which might be used to advantage in certain morbid conditions of the eye. Lapis-lazuli, another blue stone, was later substituted because of its greater intrinsic value, its similarity of color rendering it equally efficacious according to primitive ideas on this subject. When, however, in medieval times, the name sapphire came to signify the blue corundum gem known to us by this designation, the special curative virtues of the lapis-lazuli were transferred to this still more valuable stone.

[41] Labarte, "Inventaire du mobilier de Charles V," Paris, 1879, p. 308, No. 2937.

The proper method of applying a sapphire to cure plague boils is given at some length by Von Helmont. A gem of a fine, deep color was to be selected and rubbed gently and slowly around the pestilential tumor. During and immediately after this operation, the patient would feel but little alleviation; but a good while after the removal of the stone, favorable symptoms would appear, provided the malady were not too far advanced. This Von Helmont attributes to a magnetic force in the sapphire by means of which the absent gem continued to extract "the pestilential virulency and contagious poyson from the infected part."[42]

Topaz

The use of a topaz to cure dimness of vision is strongly recommended by St. Hildegard. To attain the desired end the stone was to be placed in wine and left there for three days and three nights. When retiring to sleep, the patient should rub his eyes with the moistened topaz, so that this moisture lightly touched the eyeball. After the stone had been removed, the wine could be used for five days.[43]

A Roman physician of the fifteenth century was reputed to have wrought many wonderful cures of those stricken by the plague, through touching the plague sores with a topaz which had belonged to two popes, Clement VI and Gregory II. The fact that this particular topaz had been in the hands of two supreme pontiffs must have added much to the faith reposed in the curative powers

---

[42] "A Ternary of Paradoxes, written originally by Joh. Bapt. Van Helmont and translated, illustrated, and amplicated by Walter Charleton," London, 1650, p. 17.

[43] S. Hildegardae, "Opera omnia," in Pat. Lat. ed. by J. P. Migne, vol. cxcvii, Parisiis, 1855, col. 1255.

of the stone by those upon whom it was used, and this faith may really have helped to hasten their recovery.[44]

Bloodstone

A historical instance of the use of the bloodstone to check a hemorrhage is recorded in the case of Giorgio Vasari (1514–1578), the author of the lives of the Italian painters of the Renaissance period. On a certain occasion, when the painter Luca Signorelli (1439–1521) was placing one of his pictures in a church at Arezzo, Vasari, who was present, was seized with a violent hemorrhage and fainted away. Without a moment's hesitation, Signorelli took from his pocket a bloodstone amulet and slipped it down between Vasari's shoulder-blades. The hemorrhage is said to have ceased immediately.[45]

The bloodstone was used as a remedy by the Indians of New Spain, and Monardes notes that they often cut the material into the shape of hearts. This seems a very appropriate form for an object used to check hemorrhages. The best effect was attained when the stone was first dipped in cold water and then held by the patient in his right hand. Of course the application of any cold object would serve to congeal the blood, but the connection with the heart vanishes in the direction to place the stone in the *right* hand. Monardes states that both Spaniards and Indians used the bloodstone in this way.[46]

The Franciscan friar Bernardino de Sahagun, a missionary to the Mexican Indians, shortly after the Spanish Conquest, writes that in 1576 he cured many natives who

---

[44] Arnobio, "Il tesoro delle gioie," Venice, 1602, p. 21.

[45] Bellucci, "Il feticismo in Italia," Perugia, 1907, p. 91, note.

[46] Monardes, Semplicium medicamentorum ex novo orbe delatorum historia (Latin version by Clusius), Antverpiæ, 1579, p. 51.

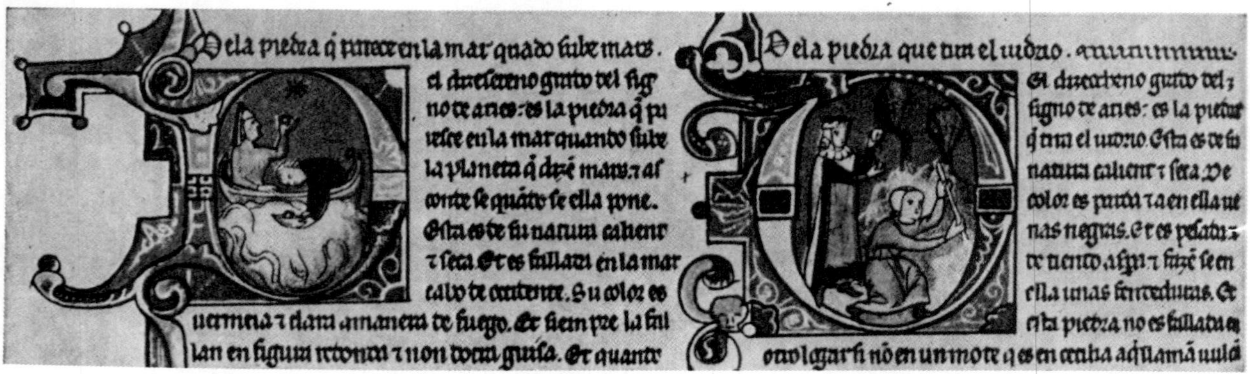

INITIALS FROM THE LAPIDARIO DE ALFONSO X (XIII CENTURY).

Codice Original (fol. 6), published in Madrid, 1881. That on the left figures "the stone found in the sea when the planet Mars rises"; that on the right, "the stone that attracts glass." Author's library.

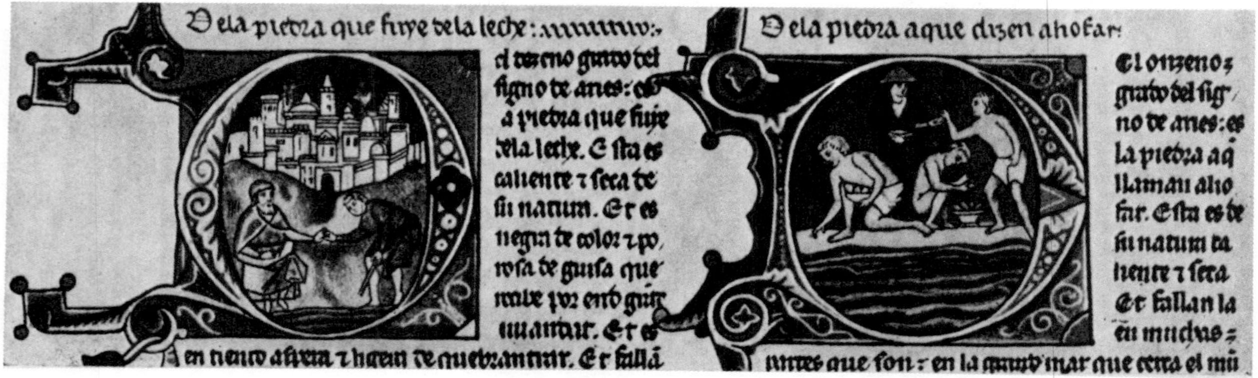

INITIALS FROM THE LAPIDARIO DE ALFONSO X.

Codice Original (fol. 4), published in Madrid, 1881. On the left, "the stone that recoils from milk"; on the right, pearl fishers

were at the point of death from hemorrhage, a result of the plague, by causing them to hold in the hand a piece of bloodstone. By this means he claims to have saved many lives.[47]

Robert Boyle, in his "Essay about the Origin and Virtues of Gems" (London, 1672, pp. 177–78), tells of a gentleman of his acquaintance who was "of a complexion extraordinary sanguin," and was much afflicted with bleeding of the nose. A gentlewoman sent to him a bloodstone, directing him to wear it suspended from his neck, and from the time he put it on he was no longer troubled with his malady. It recurred, however, if he removed the stone. When Boyle objected that this might be a result of imagination, his friend disposed of his objection by relating the instance of a woman to whom the stone had been applied when she was unconscious from loss of blood. Nevertheless, as soon as it touched her, the flow of blood was checked. Boyle states that this stone did not seem to him to resemble a true bloodstone. It may have been that the cold of the stone congealed the blood, or that the flow was checked by exhaustion.

---

[47] Sahagun, "Historia general de las cosas de Nueva España, vol. iii. Mexico, 1830, pp. 300, 301; lib. xi, cap. viii.